T0270259

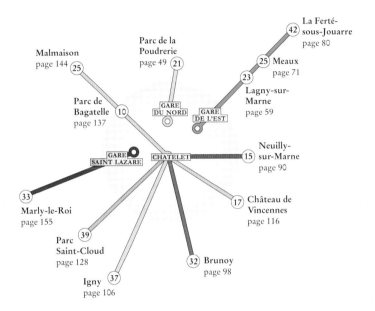

La Ferté-sous-Jouarre
page 80 — (42)

Parc de la Poudrerie
page 49 — (21)

Malmaison
page 144 — (25)

(25) Meaux
page 71

(23)

Lagny-sur-Marne
page 59

Parc de Bagatelle
page 137 — (10)

GARE DU NORD

GARE DE L'EST

Neuilly-sur-Marne
page 90 — (15)

GARE SAINT LAZARE

CHATELET

(33)

Marly-le-Roi
page 155

(17) Château de Vincennes
page 116

(39)

Parc Saint-Cloud
page 128

(32) Brunoy
page 98

Igny — (37)
page 106

Journey time in minutes from Paris by train

OISE

VEXIN FRANÇAIS

VAL D'OISE

Oise

Royaumont

Giverny

Pontoise

Auvers-sur-Oise

PARISIS

Ecouen

Mantes-la-Jolie

Seine

FRANCE

SEINE ST-DEN

Poissy

Saint-Germain-en-Laye

Malmaison

Parc de Bagatelle

Canal

Marly-le-Roi

Parc Saint-Cloud

PARIS

Vincennes

MANTOIS

YVELINES

Versailles

VAL DE M.

Jouy-en-Josas

Igny

Yvette

EURE

Rambouillet

HUREPOIX

Orge

ESSONNE

Dourdan

Essonne

Etampes

EURE-ET-LOIRE

Juine

LOIRET

KEY TO LAND USE

Urban development

Parks and Forests

Agriculture

DEPARTEMENT

Department boundary ———

HUREPOIX Pays

Île de France

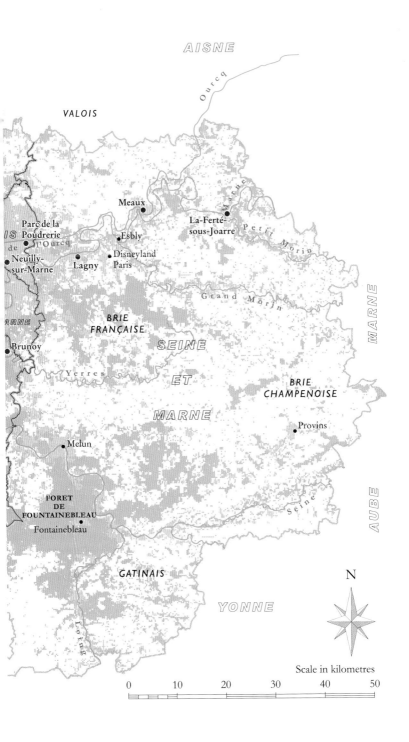

AISNE

VALOIS

Ourcq

Meaux

La-Ferté-
sous-Joarre

Petit Morin

Parc de la
Poudrerie

de Ourcq

Esbly

Neuilly-
sur-Marne

Lagny

Disneyland
Paris

MARNE

ARNE

Grand Morin

BRIE
FRANÇAISE

SEINE

Brunoy

Yerres

ET

BRIE
CHAMPENOISE

MARNE

Provins

Melun

AUBE

FORET
DE
FOUNTAINEBLEAU

Fontainebleau

Seine

GATINAIS

N

YONNE

Scale in kilometres

Loing

0   10   20   30   40   50

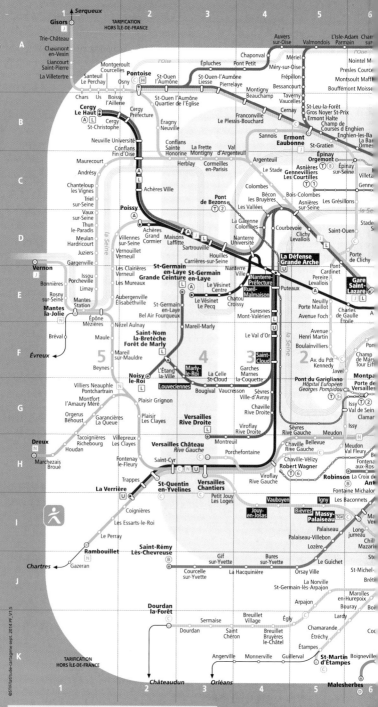

Train map of Paris and the Île de France

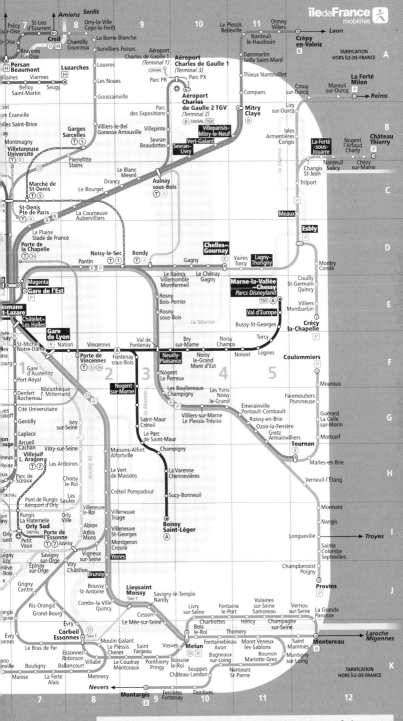

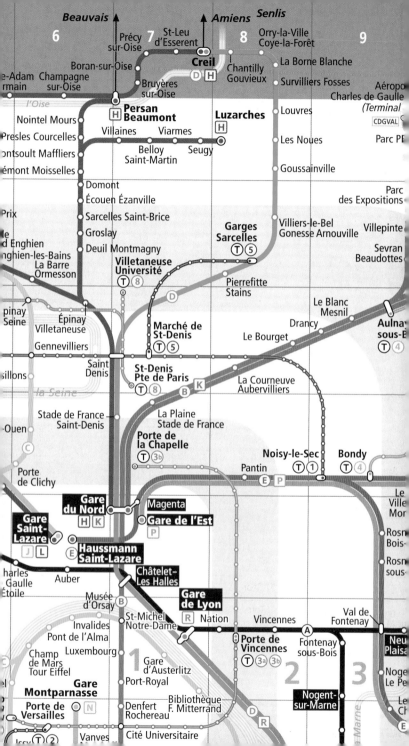

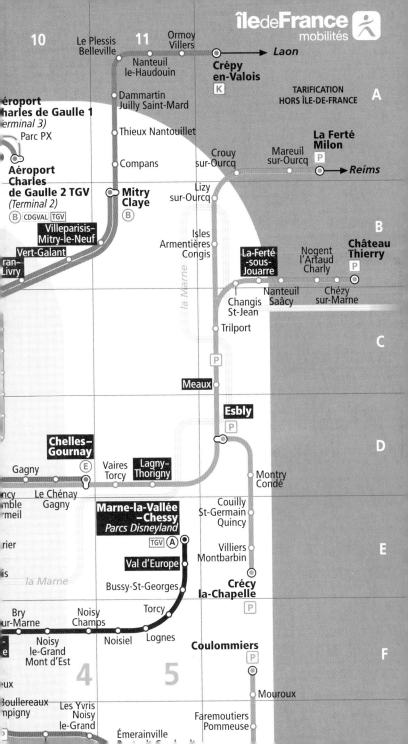

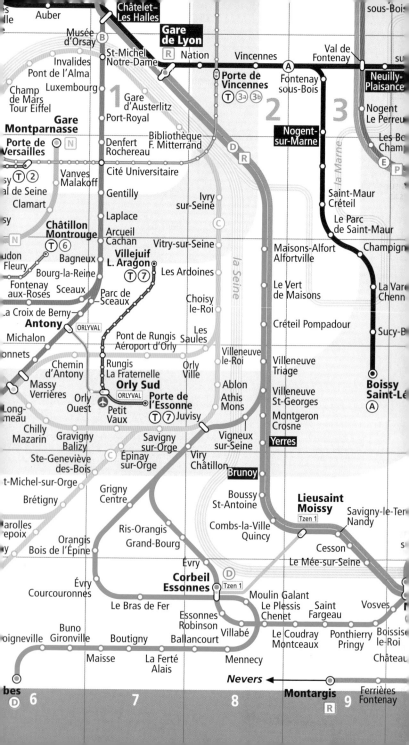

Marne

Bussy-St-Georges

Torcy

Crécy la-Chapelle
P

Noisy
Champs

Noisiel

Lognes

Coulommiers
P

Noisy
le-Grand
ont d'Est

4

5

F

Mouroux

aux

Les Yvris
Noisy
le-Grand

Faremoutiers
Pommeuse

s-sur-Marne
ssis-Trévise

Émerainville
Pontault-Combault

Roissy-en-Brie

Guérard
La Celle
sur-Morin

G

Ozoir-la-Ferrière

Gretz
Armainvilliers

Tournan
E

Mortcerf

es

Marles-en-Brie

H

uil

Verneuil-l'Étang

Mormant

Nangis

Longueville

→ *Troyes*

I

Sainte
Colombe
Septveilles

Champbenoist
Poigny

Provins
P

J

ry
eine

Fontaine
le-Port

Vulaines
sur-Seine
Samoreau

Vernou
sur-Seine

La Grande
Paroisse

Chartrettes
Bois
e-Roi

Héricy

Champagne
sur-Seine

Thomery

Saint
Mammès

Montereau
R

→ *Laroche
Migennes*

un
R

Fontainebleau
Avon

Moret Veneux
les-Sablons

Montigny
sur-Loing

Bagneaux
sur-Loing

Bourron
Marlotte Grez

uppes
ndon

Nemours
St-Pierre

**TARIFICATION
HORS ÎLE-DE-FRANCE**

K

Dordives

10

11

12

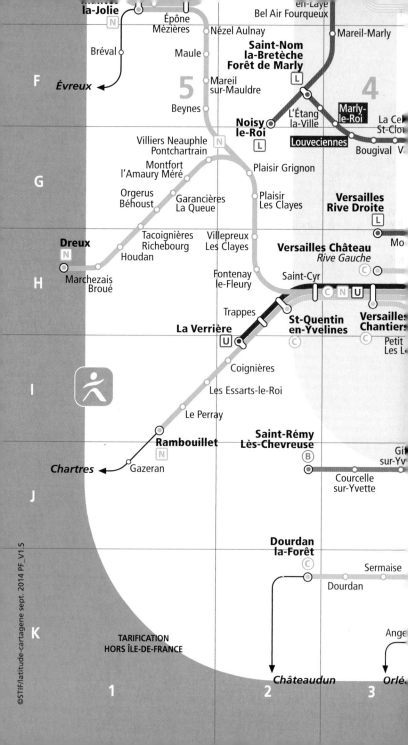

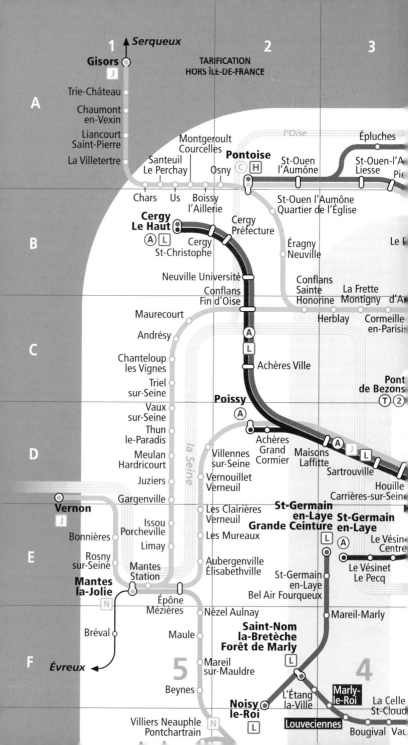

Annabel Simms

Half an Hour from Paris

Twelve secret daytrips by train

PALLAS ATHENE

Contents

Map showing journey times from Paris 1
Map of the Île de France 2
Rail map of the Île de France 4-13

Preface 23

The Île de France: past and present 29

How to use this guide 45

GARE DU NORD

1. Parc de la Poudrerie, 21 minutes by train   49
2 km walk along the Canal de l'Ourcq to astonishing remains
of 19C gunpowder factory hidden in woodland park and
nature reserve. Return from Vert-Galant station or optional
3 km continuation of canalside walk to Villeparisis station

GARE DE L'EST

2. Lagny-sur-Marne, 23 minutes by train   59
Lively medieval market town, impressive 13C church, café
with *toilettes* containing bas-relief and lavabo of 12C church,
restaurant. Optional 5 km riverside walk to monumental
open-air outdoor sculptures carved by local artist and bus to
Val d'Europe station, or 8½ km walk to sculptures returning
to Lagny along opposite bank of the Marne

Opposite: The walk from Jouarre

3. Meaux, 25 minutes by train   71
12C cathedral and Bossuet's 17C walled garden at Meaux,
restaurant, historic bridge. Optional 10 km walk along the
quiet Canal de Chalifert, past old village where Ronsard
was *curé* in 1552 and café in idyllic riverside setting, to
Esbly station

4. La Ferté-sous-Jouarre, 42 minutes by train   80
Old millstone-manufacturing town on both sides of the
River Marne, market. 6 km circular river and country walk
to well-preserved Merovingian crypts (*c.* 500-800 AD)
of Benedictine abbey at Jouarre

CHÂTELET-LES HALLES

5. Neuilly-sur-Marne, 15 minutes by train   90
1 km walk along the River Marne to 1960s *guinguette* for
drink/lunch/dancing. Return to Neuilly–Plaisance or
optional 2.8 km walk along Canal de Chelles, then bus
or 2 km walk to Chelles–Gournay station

6. Brunoy, 32 minutes by train   98
5 km walk from Brunoy along the River Yerres, past 12C
church, Neolithic menhir, island restaurant, medieval mill
and 18C bridge to country house of Impressionist painter
Caillebotte at Yerres, set in a public park by the river

7. Igny, 37 minutes by train   106
4 km walk along the River Bièvre and tea in garden of
18C Château de Roches, now a museum to Victor Hugo.
Return from Vauboyen station or optional 2½ km
continuation of country walk to Jouy-en-Josas station,
past 12C Madonna in church, Oberkampf's 18C textile
workshop, café with garden

8. Château de Vincennes, 17 minutes by métro 116
Impressive 14C castle and donjon in Bois de Vincennes,
medieval royal residence and seat of government. Good-
value traditional brasserie for lunch. Optional 3 km walk
through Bois past Lac des Minimes to the little-known
Jardin Tropical containing abandoned pavilions from the
1907 Exposition Coloniale, returning from Nogent-sur-
Marne station

9. Parc Saint-Cloud, 39 minutes by métro 128
3½ km walk from Pont de Sèvres to Musée Céramique
de Sèvres and through park, past 17C waterfall with
panoramic view of Paris. Optional visits to Musée
Historique and hilltop Jardin de Trocadéro and lake,
then downhill through old town of Saint-Cloud for
scenic return to Paris by bus

10. Parc de Bagatelle, 32 minutes by métro and bus 137
Ten-minute bus ride and short walk to landscaped
'English' park within the Bois de Boulogne with café,
lakes, grottoes, waterfalls, peacocks, roses, wild flowers
and exceptional iris garden

11. Malmaison, 25 minutes by bus 144
Bus ride and short walk to 17C Château de Malmaison,
home of Josephine and Napoleon. Optional 1½ km walk
through park to church in Rueil where Josephine is buried
and lunch in traditional brasserie, returning to La Défense
by bus. Optional continuation by bus to Bougival for
3 km walk along the Seine past Georges Bizet's house
to Rueil-Malmaison station

12. Marly-le-Roi, 33 minutes by train   155
3½ km walk through old village of Marly-le-Roi and the
park of Louis XIV's vanished château, past 17C aqueduct,
11C church and former homes of Elisabeth Vigée-Lebrun,
Pierre-Auguste Renoir and Anaïs Nin to Louveciennes
station. Optional 1 km continuation past Mme du Barry's
former château at Louveciennes, downhill to the Seine
past viewpoints painted by the Impressionists and remains
of the Machine de Marly at Bougival, returning to La
Défense by bus. Optional 1 km continuation to Pont de
Bougival past Impressionist reproductions and further
1 km optional detour uphill to village of Bougival,
returning to La Défense by bus

Getting around the Île de France   168
The cultural context   168
    Getting into the local rhythm; the pleasures of
    provincial life; the love of numbers; the French
    attitude to information
Practical details   171
    Public transport: types of ticket, trains, buses,
    taxis, boats, bicycles; walking; maps; useful
    sources of information; books, bookshops
Best days to visit   182

Glossary   184
Train traveller's glossary   186
Chronology of French rulers   187

Acknowledgements and picture credits   188

Index   189

Opposite: Stepping stones at the Parc de Bagatelle

Preface to the second edition

An Hour from Paris, a guide to 20 rewarding but little-known daytrips within an hour of Paris by train, first appeared in 2002 and is now in its third edition. I wrote the book I would have liked to have had in my hand when I first arrived in Paris from London in 1991. I needed to know how to get into the surrounding countryside by train, what was worth seeing, how long the journey would take, and how to get back without necessarily returning to my starting point. I also wanted enough local and historical information to appreciate the context of what I was seeing, a clear local map and directions, and honest comments on what I was likely to find en route, including food.

Part of my impulse to explore beyond Paris came from the need to get into the countryside and escape crowds, especially other visitors. So I also wanted to know which wild flowers and animals I might see. Ideally I wanted to be able to walk for pleasure as well as by necessity, if possible by a stream or river, but not for too long before reaching a café or a station.

No such book existed, so I started exploring the train network around Paris with a copy of the green Michelin guide to the Île de France in my hand instead. As it was written for car drivers many of its recommendations turned out to be impractical, but the places themselves were always rewarding. Some of them, such as Conflans-Sainte-Honorine, became the starting point for further explorations on foot as I began to appreciate just how interesting and accessible the Paris countryside is, and how little-known it is to most Parisians, let alone foreigners. It took several years of happy exploration and discovery before I realised that I had enough material to write the book I had always wanted to read.

The subsequent success of *An Hour from Paris* led many readers to ask for a sequel. I resisted this for some time, as their

Opposite: Porte du Cœur Volant, Parc de Marly

assumption and mine was that I would have to travel further afield to find rewarding new daytrips, probably called *Two Hours from Paris*. But when I came to look over the notes I had accumulated over 20 years, I saw that there were plenty of places in the Île de France that I had not included in *An Hour from Paris* which might be worth re-visiting, as the train service had improved so much that many of them were now far more accessible. I did re-visit them, over several years, and was delighted to make further discoveries, such as the country walks around Auvers-sur-Oise. Meanwhile Paris friends kept giving me ideas for new destinations within an hour of Paris, such as Marly-le-Roi and the Parc de la Poudrerie, and I discovered others myself, such as the Canal de Chalifert at Meaux. Finally I decided to put ten of these trips taking around half an hour by train into a shorter book called *Half an Hour from Paris*.

Of the twelve destinations described in this new edition, the oldest ones with Roman or medieval origins, Lagny, Meaux and La Ferté-sous-Jouarre, are to the east of Paris where few tourists go, as are the most surprising places to be found just outside Paris: the Château de Vincennes, the Parc de la Poudrerie and Neuilly-sur-Marne. Brunoy to the south is also of medieval origin, whereas Igny in the south and Parc de Bagatelle, Parc de Saint-Cloud, Malmaison and Marly-le-Roi in the west developed between the 17th and 19th centuries mainly as a result of their proximity to Versailles. Today they are prosperous suburbs concealing an interesting history, but little known to foreign visitors.

Although there is now far more information about the Île de France available than there was when I first started exploring, these lesser-known places tend to be mentioned superficially or not at all. Not everything is available online, and even if it is, it often helps to know beforehand exactly what you are looking for. The medieval stone bas-relief of St Furcy in the *toilettes* of the Café St Furcy at Lagny is not mentioned by the tourist office and the locals do not spare it a glance, although I did find it on an obscure website once I had discovered its existence. And Google does not go into detail on how to get to places like the Parc de la Poudrerie

Opposite: Merovingian crypt with Roman pillars, Jouarre

by train or pick out the most rewarding route for walkers when they get there.

In revising *Half An Hour From Paris* for this second edition, I have observed that this situation has not fundamentally changed since the book was first published in 2018. Despite the greater accessibility and awareness of places close to Paris as a result of the Grand Paris initiative, Parisians do not see their local countryside with the same eyes as a foreigner. I am happy to report that the bas-relief of St Furcy in the café at Lagny is still ignored by the tourist office and the locals, although there is now a new footbridge across the Marne which extends the options for the suggested walk. In fact, there are more recommended walks in the Île de France accessible by public transport available from various French sources than ever before, but their focus still tends to be specialised—historical, architectural, botanical, cultural or sporty. The ambling walker who is curious about everything and happy to stop at a café or restaurant is not particularly catered for and practical information on how to get there and back by public transport remains minimal.

Apart from a few improvements, additions and updates, surprisingly little has changed in the original ten places included in this book. I have added two new chapters, the Parc Saint-Cloud to the west and Brunoy to the south east, to even out the circle of places around Paris which was rather biased towards the north east and because I think these destinations are good value.

The thrill of discovering places like these a stone's throw from Paris is what makes exploration off the beaten track so rewarding. I hope that you will enjoy these trips as much as I have enjoyed discovering and researching them.

This edition is dedicated to Joan Fleming, my helpful, amusing and intrepid companion on so many of these walks.

Opposite: Cheval de Marly, Parc de Marly

The Île de France: past and present

*Place-names in **bold** are described in the text*

A foreigner's first impressions

When I first came to live in Paris I was puzzled by the phrase 'Île de France' (the 'island of France'). I gradually realised that it referred to the area around Paris for a radius of about 80 kilometres (I was vague about this) and that *les Franciliens*, 'the islanders of France', meant the inhabitants of this region. Rather like Greater London, except that no one talks about Greater Londoners. I did not realise that the Île de France is almost eight times the size of Greater London, with a much better train service.

Beyond noticing that it seemed to contain a lot of famous places, which I felt slightly guilty about not wanting to visit (Versailles, Fontainebleau, Barbizon), I had no clear idea of it as a region, nor did I feel the need for one. When I thought of the French countryside, I thought of the South of France, the Auvergne, the Loire, Burgundy, Brittany and, at a pinch, Normandy, which really seemed too close to England to count.

I also began to think of the area around Paris as the *banlieue* (a much more negative word than 'suburb') with an authentically Parisian shudder of fear, pity or contempt. My Paris, *real* Paris, did not extend beyond zone one of the *Carte Orange*, now replaced by the *Passe Navigo*, the métro and bus pass covering up to five zones around Paris. The limits of Zone One are still those of the old city boundary, traceable by the circle of métro stations beginning with the word *Porte*, indicating the entrance gates that were once part of the walls surrounding the city. I had assumed that these gates had disappeared

Opposite: The remains of a 13th-century church in the toilettes *of the Brasserie Saint Furcy, Lagny-sur-Marne*

in the Middle Ages and was amused to hear Parisians referring to a place as being *intra muros*, 'within the walls'. Clearly, these walls still existed in people's imaginations, confirming my view that Paris was essentially a charmed circle enclosing all that was civilised and that the *banlieue*, a desert of concrete containing dreary new industries and inhabited by philistines, began just outside the gates. In fact, the fortifications surrounding the city were only demolished in 1919 and have been effectively replaced by the *boulevard péripherique* (ring road), which explains the pervasiveness of this mind-set and the rapidity with which I picked it up.

Like most visitors, I was really only familiar with the fifth *arrondissement*, the Latin Quarter. I had to gradually extend my mental map of the city to include the other 19 *arrondissements*, all beginning with the postcode 75 and therefore *intra muros*. Meanwhile, my job as a teacher of business English was forcing me to make forays outside these walls into what Parisians called *la proche banlieue* (inner suburbs) where many businesses and business schools are located. I travelled to La Défense and Cergy to the west, Noisy-le-Grand and Bussy-St-Georges to the east and Evry to the south. I found the modern architecture of these places dismayingly soulless, pitied the people who actually lived there and cursed the excellence of the public transport system which made them all too accessible from Paris, depriving me of an excuse not to go there.

At the same time, I was learning to adapt to the endless succession of public holidays the French enjoy—among the highest number in Europe. Almost every month is punctuated by at least one and suddenly Paris empties as people decide they will *faire le pont*: 'bridge' the official holiday to the weekend by taking the days in between as additional holiday. They go skiing or mushroom-picking, redecorate the house or head for their relatives or *résidences secondaires* in the country. As a newly arrived, under-paid expatriate, none of these options seemed to be available to me (I didn't even know where to look for the mushrooms) but there was no work for me in Paris and the urge to get into the countryside, *any* countryside, if only for a day, would become irresistibly strong at these times.

Le Grand Miroir, Parc de Marly

So, armed with my *Carte Orange* and the green Michelin guide to the Île de France, I found myself getting on the suburban trains outside working hours, determined to make the most of what was, after all, on my doorstep. I soon discovered that the efficiency of the commuter network surrounding Paris had its positive side—the stately 17th-century parks of Sceaux, **Marly-le-Roi** and **Saint-Cloud** were easily accessible and a world away from the shopping centres, flats and offices of places like Noisy-le-Grand and Evry. Encouraged, I began to go further afield, to *la grande banlieue* (the outer suburbs): Versailles, St-Germain-en-Laye, Chevreuse, Rambouillet, Chantilly and Senlis and became gradually aware of a whole rich hinterland of old towns and villages, châteaux, parks and forests surrounding Paris, extending for up to 80 kilometres to the south and east, 32 kilometres to the north and 56 kilometres to the west, the limits of the Île de France railway network.

The two faces of the Île de France: the old and the new

In fact, there seemed to be two Îles de France: the pastoral region evoked by the names of the old *pays* mentioned in Michelin, accessible to car-drivers, and the modern *banlieue* served by the SNCF and divided into new and meaningless *départements* with unfamiliar postcodes. Not possessing a car, I was forced to superimpose one map on the other and gradually discovered that the modern administrative region had grown out of the historic, pastoral one and that in many places they exist side by side. I began to look at the horrible places where I had to work with new eyes. For example, Bussy-St-Georges, close to Disneyland, is a new business, educational and residential complex, tastefully planned and quite lifeless. The little village of Bussy-St-Georges, a long walk from the new RER (express suburban train) station, pre-dates it by several centuries, perhaps a millennium, and belongs to a different world. It is inseparable from the surrounding countryside, the old Brie region where the famous cheese is made, just as the modern complex of the same name spiritually belongs to the new town of Marne-la-Vallée and the RER station, without which it could not exist.

Yet both are typical of the complicated historical relationship between Paris and the Île de France, which has been variously neglected, feared, nourished or exploited by the capital. At this stage, however, my mental map of the Île de France was still largely formed by the Michelin guide and I had only the dimmest notions of the places it *doesn't* mention and of the context in which I was living and working. I had just about heard of 'red' working-class suburbs like St-Denis and Sarcelles to the north and of the new towns of Cergy-Pontoise, St-Quentin-en-Yvelines, Evry, Melun-Sénart and Marne-la-Vallée encircling Paris. Indeed, I had worked in Evry and never wanted to go there again.

But I was becoming more adventurous as I became more knowledgeable about the train network. I began to go to places to the north and east of Paris which hardly rated a mention in Michelin, attracted by the **Canal de l'Ourcq** and the **River Marne**. They were less elegant than the prosperous suburbs

Guinguette Chez Fifi, Neuilly-sur-Marne

to the west of Paris, but I sensed the continuity of a popular culture there, which I found unexpected and attractive. Their 1950s atmosphere, which reminded me of all the old black and white French films I had seen in London, was in fact older than I thought, often associated with a working river or canal and the tradition of eating, drinking, dancing and generally having a good time by the water. In fact, by taking the train on a Sunday to places like the *guinguette* (a traditional riverside restaurant where people go to dance) at **Neuilly-sur-Marne**, I was unconsciously following an old Parisian tradition: using the transport routes which follow the network of rivers surrounding the city as an escape from the pressures of living in it.

A weekend escape for Parisians, past and present

Gradually I became aware of the persistence of other traditions, national as well as local, bourgeois as well as popular. But the most obvious one, shared by all social classes, is the Parisian habit of using the rural parts of the Île de France as a kind of weekend playground, a countryside refuge from the stress and pollution of the city. Picturesque places easily accessible from

An FFRP walker's sign (see pp. 177-178)

Paris, like Yerres (**Brunoy**), Louveciennes (**Marly-le-Roi**) or Jouy-en-Josas (**Igny**), used to contain almost as many weekend residents as permanent ones, before modern transport made more exotic locations easily accessible. Successful writers, artists, musicians and politicians all bought country houses in the Île de France. The dense scattering of châteaux around Paris, the richest concentration in France outside the Loire valley, was the older, aristocratic version of the same impulse. No one with any ambition, then or now, could afford to be too far away from Paris, which has always been the cultural and economic as well as the administrative and political capital of the country.

The 20th-century decline of the traditional industries of the North and of St Etienne has been followed by the emergence of new high-tech industries, concentrated—where else?—in the area closest to Paris. So, despite efforts to relieve the pressure on the capital by building new towns around it, it is still the most densely populated city in Europe and the urge to escape from it into the surrounding countryside has remained as strong as ever.

Although pollution in Paris increased dramatically with the advent of the car, there is also nothing new about Parisian awareness of it. The impulse to breathe fresh air and renew contact with rural roots can be seen in the weekend invasion of the Forest of Fontainebleau by amateur rock-climbers, by the number of ramblers' associations affiliated to the FFRP (Féderation Française de la Randonnée Pedestre) and by the existence of countless other groups who go cycling, riding or bird-watching in the forests of the Île de France. There is even a group which specialises in mushroom excursions in the autumn, when the more accessible forests are regularly denuded by enthusiastic amateurs.

The triumphant survival of the countryside: some surprising statistics

In spite of all this urban invasion, the Île de France remains remarkably untamed, by English Home Counties standards. I saw my first snake (harmless, I was assured by my shrugging French companions) on a bird-watching excursion less than 60 kilometres north of Paris and was horrified when they identified the droppings of a wild boar nearby. I had to take their word for it that boars leave you alone if you leave them alone and, judging by the speedy disappearance of the snake and the invisibility of the boar, the wildlife does seem to be more frightened of us than we are of it. I have also noticed that wild flowers and birds that are rare in England are commonplace in the Île de France, not to mention the carpets of wild strawberries that no one bothers to pick.

The reason for the survival of authentic countryside around Paris is that, although the Île de France is the most heavily and densely populated region in the country with 12.2 million inhabitants, almost a fifth of the total population of France, this

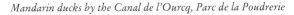

Mandarin ducks by the Canal de l'Ourcq, Parc de la Poudrerie

Canal de Chalifert towpath, near Meaux

population is very unevenly distributed. Only 20 per cent of
the total surface area of 12,000 square kilometres is completely urbanised, concentrated in a radius of about 30 kilometres
around Paris, while 23 per cent is still forest and 50 per cent is
agricultural. And even within the 30-kilometre radius, there are
unexpected pockets of greenery, such as **Brunoy**, **Malmaison**,
Marly-le-Roi, **Igny** and **Neuilly-sur-Marne**, as well as the two
great wooded parks to the east and west of Paris, the Bois de
Vincennes and the Bois de Boulogne. The most surprising of the
parks described in this book is the **Parc de la Poudrerie**, 18 kilometres from Paris, separated from a densely populated suburb
by the Canal de l'Ourcq, where you can see wood anemones,
mandarin ducks and red squirrels flourishing in deep woodland
and hear the tapping of woodpeckers in ancient trees.

In fact, although the population density of Paris is four
times that of Inner London, the situation is more than reversed
for the surrounding countryside, the density in Greater London
being almost ten times that of the Île de France. Beyond *la proche
banlieue* huge tracts of land are given over to intensive agriculture, and it is possible to walk for miles without seeing more than
a handful of people. This can be the case even in places which are

only around half an hour from Paris by train, such as the walk along the Canal de Chalifert from **Meaux**, along the Marne from **Lagny** or across country to **La Ferté-sous-Jouarre**.

Why the kingdom of France began in the Île de France

The name of the region itself provides the clue. Why is it called an island when it is nearly 160 kilometres from the sea, and why 'France' when it covers less than three per cent of the surface area of modern France? The region takes its name from the rich grain-producing plateau around St-Denis to the north of Paris, the old *Pays de France*, sometimes referred to as the *Plaine de France*. It is an 'island' in the sense that it is encircled by three rivers – the Seine, the Marne, and the Oise. However, the term 'Île de France' has always referred to the area around Paris rather than to a geographically or culturally distinct region, such as Brittany, for example. Its administrative boundaries have been shifting since the Middle Ages, shrinking to a radius of 30 kilometres around Paris or expanding for up to 100 kilometres from the centre. The current boundaries were only fixed in 1976. As an official term, 'Île de France' is not recorded before 1519, although it was probably in use earlier. By that date the rulers of this once tiny but prosperous region had consolidated their power to such an extent that their kingdom of 'France' included almost the whole of the country.

The reasons for the gradual emergence of the rulers of Paris as the dominant political power in the country are ultimately geographical. The city, first mentioned by Caesar in 53 BC, was established on the Île de la Cité, where the passage across the Seine was easiest. It is at the heart of a low-lying region surrounded by rivers. A natural crossroads, it allowed navigable access to the sea and to northern Europe, as well as to central and south-eastern France. The importance of river transport in a region of uncleared forest was crucial; a boat has always featured in the heraldry of the city and now forms the official logo of the City of Paris. The rich, silty soil of the region and its mixed continental and oceanic climate also favoured the early

Canal de Chelles, Neuilly-sur-Marne

development of agriculture. The growth of its capital stimulated demand for its produce, attracting migrants from poorer parts of the country. The symbiosis between Paris and its setting, the growth of the city depending on the prosperity and accessibility of the region and vice versa, can be seen by glancing at any map of modern transport routes, which follow the old routes formed by the river valleys, all converging on Paris.

However, the political importance of the region and its capital fluctuated considerably following the collapse of Roman rule. Lyon had been the capital of Gaul under the Romans, but in 508 Paris became the official capital of Clovis the Frank. It was the election of Hugues Capet, Count of Paris and Duke of France, as their leader by his fellow-nobles at Senlis in 987 that really marked the beginning of the political power of Paris and its region, and of the history of modern France.

How fragile and uncertain this power was can be seen by a glance at the political map of France for six centuries after 987. The ninth-century Viking invasions from Normandy were followed by invasions by their descendants, the kings of England, in alliance with the dukes of Burgundy, not to mention the threat of invasion by the Holy Roman Emperors in Germany. The king of France, ringed by powerful neighbours in England, Germany, Italy and Spain, was only the nominal leader of vassals whose territories were much bigger than his: Normandy, Brittany, Burgundy, Aquitaine, Toulouse, Anjou and Provence. The English were only driven out in the 15th century and the country did not become fully unified under the kings of France until the late 16th century, with the ending of the Wars of Religion. The old towns described in this book, **Brunoy**, **Lagny-sur-Marne**, **Meaux** and **La Ferté-sous-Jouarre**, all had ramparts for a good reason and the **Château de Vincennes** is still a fortress.

Passage de l'Arcade, part of the former ramparts at Lagny-sur-Marne

The ambiguous relationship between Paris and its province

Despite constant attacks, the agricultural prosperity and stability of the region and its relatively high population, stimulated by the growth of Paris, enabled its rulers to gradually impose their power on the neighbouring provinces. However, their relationship with their own province was, and remains, ambiguous.

The reorganisation of the region in 1976 was a belated attempt to come to terms with a century of unplanned suburban development, in the course of which the rapidly expanding population of Paris had overflowed into *la triste banlieue*. The five new towns, conceived of as centres in their own right, rather than as dormitories of Paris, date from this period. So does the building of the RER express train network going deep into the countryside, the linking of six motorways to the *boulevard périphérique*, the construction of the Charles de Gaulle airport at Roissy and the relocation of research and higher educational establishments from Paris to the Île de France.

As a result of these improved transport links many picturesque old towns have successfully absorbed new immigrant populations. You might see a mixed black and white congregation in the ancient church, Turkish fast food outlets in the main street, a Moroccan-owned *alimentation* (general grocer) and a *café-tabac* run by a Chinese family. Indeed, without these new residents, the chances of getting a drink or a snack on Sundays in some of these little towns would be zero.

But despite these examples of successful integration and the attempts to rationalise the growth of Paris and to develop a coherent policy for the whole region, the persistence of the traditional '*Paris-province*' split, so typical of the rest of France, is still striking, at any rate to a Londoner. Although it accounts for less than one per cent of the surface area of the Île de France, the City of Paris is still a *département* in its own right, and its former mayor, Jacques Chirac, was president of France for 12 years. Transport links have traditionally bypassed connections between the suburbs in favour of serving the Paris hub. Provincial distrust of the power and arrogance of Paris seems to be shared by some of the inhabitants of its own region and this distrust is

A view of western Paris from the chemin de la Machine, Louveciennes

returned with interest by many Parisians. Despite the re-naming of the suburban train network on the departure boards of Paris stations as *Île de France* rather than *Banlieue*, many Parisians do not travel there unless they have to, and are more familiar with Normandy, Guadeloupe, New York or London than they are with their own countryside. And although five times more people live in the *banlieue* than in Paris itself, they too tend not to explore the Île de France beyond their particular part of it.

The 21st century: Greater Paris

At the beginning of the 20th century, the fear was that the explosive growth of Paris would engulf the Île de France, turning the entire region into a megalopolis. This has not happened. Since the 1960s the falling national birth rate and improved educational opportunities beyond the capital have affected population growth in the Île de France. It has been gradual, rather than explosive. The population of Paris is 2.2 million, compared to 2.9 million in 1921, partly as a result of the success of the new towns and the transport infrastructures created after 1976. The population of the Île de France, Paris included, is 12.2 million rather than the 14 million anticipated in the 1960s and is now expected to reach 12.7 million by 2030.

But the traditionally negative Parisian attitude to the *banlieue* was dramatically endorsed in October and November 2005, when the poorer immigrant suburbs close to Paris were swept by riots, which quickly spread to similar suburbs in other parts of France. Both the size of these suburbs and the crime rate are one tenth of those in American cities, but the unrest acted as a wake-up call to the authorities. More recently, so did the fact that some of the perpetrators of the Paris terrorist attacks in November 2015 were young men who had grown up in the poorer suburbs close to Paris. But there was already a growing recognition that the division between Paris *intra-muros* and the rest of the region was neither sustainable nor desirable. One immediate result of the 2005 riots was the acceleration of the demolition programme for the 1960s concrete tower blocks in the *proche banlieue* and the realisation that something needed to be done urgently to tackle the chronic housing shortage in the region and prevent Paris from turning into a 'museum city'.

In 2007 President Sarkozy announced his project *Le Grand Paris*, a complete rethink of the future development of Paris which would bring its relationship with its immediate region into line with that of other world cities, such as New York, London and Tokyo. New transport infrastructures would be created, linking suburb to suburb rather than converging on Paris. This would in turn encourage the growth of 'clusters of excellence', for example, a kind of French Silicon Valley in the south-western plateau of Saclay. The number of new homes being built would double to 70,000 a year. These plans were endorsed by the succeeding Socialist government, leading to the creation in 2016 of a new administrative structure, *Métropole du Grand Paris*, consisting of Paris and the most densely urbanised areas surrounding it for around 30 kilometres, home to ten million people.

Existing RER and métro lines are now being progressively improved and extended and new bus and tram routes added.

Four new métro lines, linking the suburbs without passing through Paris, and an express line between the Gare de l'Est and Charles De Gaulle airport are being built, to be completed by 2030. The new train map will look more like the Tube map of London or the subway map of New York, with no obvious magic circle separating the city from the region and a more evenly distributed transport network. The stated aim of the project is to reduce inequalities in wealth and density between the prosperous suburbs west of Paris and the poorer ones close to Paris in the north and east, as well as between Paris and the Île de France, by vastly improving public transport, renovating neglected areas and building new homes that are energy-efficient. The region's huge tracts of agricultural land, forest and green spaces will be protected and its cultural riches promoted. One small but visible result of this policy is that the screens on the smart new suburban trains which are rapidly replacing the older stock now feature continuous footage of the historic and cultural landmarks en route. Another is the growing use of the term 'Grand Paris' or 'Paris Region' to replace 'Île de France' in official nomenclature. The capping at 5€ of the price of a train ticket from Paris to anywhere in the Île de France in March 2022 is the most recent attempt to extend the benefits of this dynamic region to all its inhabitants.

It is impossible yet to say how these changes will play out. One result of modernisation in the Île de France has been standardisation and the spread of a depressing blandness as the architecture changes, owners of family-run cafés and restaurants retire and fast-food outlets take their place. Some picturesque old places on the periphery seem in full decline and some postcard-pretty old villages with prosperous inhabitants have become sterile residential enclaves. In both cases, there are few inhabitants visible on Sundays and no cafés open, if they exist at all. Improved public transport links and the greater economic opportunities that come with them could breathe new life into such places and change the distressing tendency of modest family-owned cafés and restaurants to close down for want of local, i.e. not car-borne, customers. And if the social tension in the poorer suburbs is eased by a fairer distribution of housing,

Front entrance facing the River Marne of the Hotel Île-des-Cygnes on the canal de Chalifert

jobs, transport and public amenities, that can only be a good thing for everyone, residents and visitors alike.

Meanwhile, I put my faith in the continuity of the traditional *savoir vivre* rooted deep in the French psyche, the quality which first drew me, like so many other visitors, to France. This quality, and the social harmony that seems to go with it, are still tangible in the old towns of the Île de France which have modernised but kept their character, such as **Lagny-sur-Marne**, and even in unlikely suburbs close to Paris, such as Villeparisis near the **Parc de la Poudrerie**.

I continue to discover places where local people, some of them immigrants, are happy to share the traditional French enjoyment of life with appreciative visitors, such as the café on the Canal de Chalifert near **Meaux** or the *guinguette* at **Neuilly-sur-Marne**. In fact, I have experienced the Frenchness of France more often in the Île de France, where the slower pace lends itself more easily to savouring the moment, than in Paris.

With the help of this book, which still only scratches the surface of the countryside around Paris, I hope that you will enjoy discovering it for yourself.

How to use this guide: quick reference

The visits are arranged by station of departure, moving clockwise from the Gare du Nord, then by journey time by train, starting with the shortest. See the **Contents** page for an overview. All visits begin at the local railway station, where it is suggested that you park if you are arriving by car. Information on public transport in the Île de France can be found on p. 171.

If you are going by train, the only essential **map** is the RATP *Plan de Réseau Île de France (no. 1)*, see p. 178. A smaller version of it is reproduced at the front of this book. You should also read the section on trains on pp. 173-176. For drivers, the most useful map to take is Michelin no. 106, *Environs de Paris* (see p. 178).

Each of the twelve visits ends with a boxed summary of essential information to help you decide at a glance if the visit is practical. The summary is followed by details of how to get there, when to go, other useful information such as admission times and prices, and brief details, sometimes recommendations, of local restaurants and cafés.

The **Navigo Zone** in the inset box refers to the zones covered by the Navigo travel pass, which are shown on the railway map at the front of this book.

The **frequency of trains** depends on when you are travelling, but is generally at least hourly and usually half-hourly or less. There are more trains during weekday rush hours and there might be fewer on Sunday mornings but more on Sunday evenings. Some train timetables change slightly every summer and winter, usually by a few minutes, but not all trains are affected. For this reason, the information on trains under the heading 'Getting there' gives the frequency of trains, which hardly ever changes, rather than the timetables, which might. If weekends are not mentioned, this means that there is no change in frequency from the weekday service. For detailed up to date information on train times you should check with the SNCF (see p. 174).

The times of the last train back in the 'Getting there' section and the opening times in the 'When to go' section may affect your plans. Check the table **Best days to visit** on p. 182-183 for a summary of which museums and châteaux are open on which days. Opening hours, and other things too, change all the time, so the details given under 'Useful information' may be out of date. If you have chosen a visit because of a particular attraction, **always phone first** to make sure it is still available and open on the day and at the time you plan to go.

Journey time in the inset box refers to the time spent in the train. To work out the time you should allow for a visit, check the inset box for the distances between two places and also look at the scale of the local map. If an **alternative return** station is given, you have the choice of returning to Paris from the station you arrived at or of walking to the alternative station. It takes about an hour to walk three to five kilometres (two to three miles), depending on whether you are a slow or a brisk walker. The half or full day suggested in 'Length of visit' is a rough guide. Generally, a half day is the minimum you should allow, which would become a full day if you included certain options, such as a walk to an alternative station.

In general

French words likely to be unfamiliar to an English reader are followed by a translation in brackets. There is also a glossary of the French words most frequently used in the text on p. 184 and a train traveller's glossary on p. 186. However, I have not translated the basic words which you would find in a general phrase-book or dictionary, to avoid irritating readers who speak French.

All **distances** in the inset box are given in kilometres first, as this is how the information will be presented on road signs, and then in miles. One mile = 1.6 km, one km = 0.6 miles.

Teachers and journalists from all countries may be entitled to **free or reduced admission** to some state-run museums or monuments, but this generous French quirk is rarely publicised.

Chemin de la Machine at Bougival

It is always worth taking proof of your professional status with you and asking 'Est-ce qu'il y a un tarif réduit pour les professeurs/la presse?' There is usually a reduction for children, students and people aged under 26 or over 60. Again, take a student card or passport with you.

It is quicker and cheaper to **buy your train tickets at a métro station**, as a métro journey is always included in the price of tickets to the Île de France. There is no advantage in buying a return ticket, which costs the same as two singles, but if you have a Navigo Découverte pass for Paris (Zones 1-2) travel to Zones 3-5 is free. Even if you don't have a Navigo, travel to Zones 1-5 is now capped at 5€. See p. 172.

It is not essential to have read the 'Getting around' section (pp. 168-181), nor the chapter on the Île de France before going on any of these trips, although you might find them interesting to browse through in the train. They are intended as helpful background information, likely to be of special interest to those readers who have developed a taste for exploring and want to branch out on their own.

1. Parc de la Poudrerie

**The astonishing remains of a 19th-century gunpowder
factory in deep woodland by a canal close to Paris**

I was shown the Parc de la Poudrerie by a Paris friend who used
to live nearby. Only locals seem to know about it and, as it is in a
densely populated suburb not far from Clichy-sous-Bois where
the 2005 Paris riots started, I was completely unprepared for the
mysterious and beautiful experience it turned out to be. Within
five minutes of leaving the station you are in another world,
where the tranquil canal mirrors the reflections of the trees and
sky, disturbed only by the passage of a pair of exotic mandarin
ducks or the scurrying of a water vole. Violets, primroses and
cowslips grow along the towpath. A little further on, the dignified brick and stone remains of the abandoned gunpowder
factory above the canal blend harmoniously into the ancient
woodland which makes up a large part of the 137 hectare park,
full of wood anemones and bluebells in spring and the tapping
sound of woodpeckers. It is listed as of outstanding natural interest because the deliberately scattered buildings, laid out in a
fan shape to minimise damage in case of an accidental explosion,
and the undisturbed woodland containing a variety of ancient
trees and three ponds, have favoured species such as butterflies,
weasels, red squirrels, pipistrelle bats, newts, salamanders, bea-
vers, woodpeckers and falcons which are not usually found in
urban areas. About 30 of the original 300 buildings have been
saved from demolition, one housing a small technical museum,
and another used for temporary exhibitions.

The park is popular with local families as well as nature-
lovers, as it has something for everybody: romantically decaying buildings emerging from the trees, a *buvette*, cycle paths, a

Opposite: Parc de la Poudrerie

museum and an exhibition centre, surrounded by undisturbed woodland and ponds. Best of all, it is next to the canal and the railway so it is possible to prolong the peaceful towpath walk and return to Paris in under half an hour from one of the three RER stations beside the Canal de l'Ourcq.

The 'Poudrerie Nationale'

The deep woodland at Sevran, part of an ancient forest close to Paris, the canal and the railway, offered an excellent sparsely-populated site for the state-owned factory making potentially dangerous explosives. The woodland and the canal effectively isolated it and the canal provided water for the steam-driven machines as well as transport for the raw materials. The factory operated from 1873 to 1973, when most of it was demolished as part of a rationalisation plan after the signing of the Treaty of Rome in 1957. At the peak of its activity in 1914 the Poudrerie Nationale employed over 3,000 workers, producing 28 tonnes of gunpowder daily. In 1944 the 'poudriers' clandestinely made explosives for the Resistance while the factory was occupied by the Germans. The abandoned site has been a public park since 1982 but is little-known outside the local area.

Suggested 2 km canalside walk to the Parc de la Poudrerie

From the **station** at Sevran-Livry follow the signs for 'Sortie place de la Gare'. Cross the square up to the bridge and turn left along the canal. Turn sharp left to join the towpath and follow it to the right for a kilometre until you come to a footbridge signposted 'Pont de la Poudrerie'. This is the quietest and most beautiful part of the canal walk, where you are likely only to meet an occasional fisherman or stroller. Meadowsweet, butter-cups, violets, cowslips and primroses grow here in spring and mauve wild orchids grow on the even less-frequented opposite bank. It is here that you are most likely to glimpse a water vole or see a *ragondin*, 'coypu' in English, a South American import

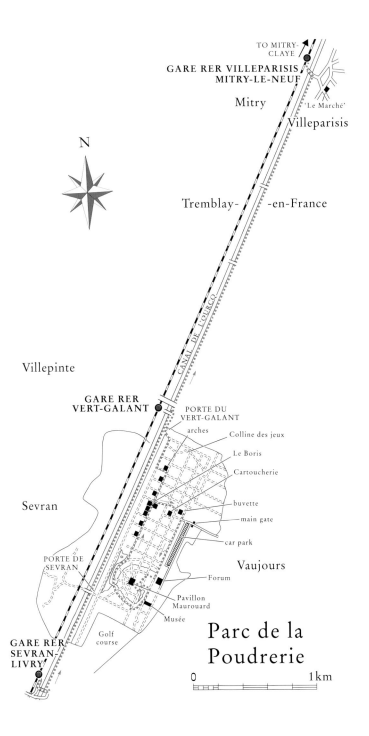

TO MITRY-CLAYE

GARE RER VILLEPARISIS MITRY-LE-NEUF

Mitry

'Le Marché'

Villeparisis

Tremblay- -en-France

CANAL DE L'OURCQ

Villepinte

GARE RER VERT-GALANT

PORTE DU VERT-GALANT

arches

Colline des jeux

Le Boris

Cartoucherie

buvette

main gate

car park

Sevran

Vaujours

PORTE DE SEVRAN

Forum

Pavillon Maurouard

Musée

GARE RER SEVRAN-LIVRY

Golf course

Parc de la Poudrerie

0   1km

which looks like a beaver with a smaller tail. It was introduced into France a century ago to be bred for its fur. Another introduced species which has escaped into the wild is the colourful mandarin duck, which is quite common on this part of the canal, swimming alongside the native mallards.

You could enter the park from the **Pont de la Poudrerie**, where there are steps just before the footbridge leading up to the Porte de Sevran entrance to the park, but I have found it more rewarding to continue along this quiet beautiful stretch of the canal to the Porte du Vert-Galant, from where you enter the park more impressively through one of the ex-factory arches. If you do enter the park at the Porte de Sevran, the map just inside the gates shows the Pont de la Poudrerie as 'Pont de l'Ourcq'.

When you reach the next bridge, the **Passerelle du Vert-Galant**, you will see that it is in fact two bridges, a footbridge and a road bridge behind it. Go under the footbridge and round to the right onto the uphill path parallel to the canal, which is signposted 'Parc Forestier de la Poudrerie'. At the top of the path go through the Porte du Vert-Galant into the park. Follow the path downhill and at the bottom you will see a map.

Turn right along the straight main cycle path and follow it for a little way. At the third turning on the left you will see a handsome red brick and stone arch in the near distance, one of six which are strung out in a row, parallel to the main path. They were constructed around 1880 to carry overhead steel cables operated by pulleys which transmitted steam power to the factory workshops where the gunpowder was produced. Follow the path through the arch and turn right, passing more arches on your right until you come to an imposing but decaying building straddling the path, labelled **Le Boris**. It housed the machines where steam power was produced for transmission to the vanished factory buildings and the plaque explains that it is named after one of the engineers who worked there.

Retrace your steps and turn right from 'Le Boris' to follow the worn rail lines embedded in the ground and the sign **'Accueil-buvette'** which will eventually lead you past another imposing building on the right, 'La Cartoucherie' where black

Le Boris

gunpowder was produced, to a grassy space with a little drinks stand with tables and sunshades outside and *les toilettes.*

From the *buvette,* with the Cartoucherie behind you, continue to the next broad straight path and turn right. Continue past a children's playground, the 'Ferme Pédagogique' containing noisy geese, the 'Forum' and the 'Maison des Amis du Parc' on the left, where there is a kind of crossroads.

Take the middle path and follow it diagonally across the grass to the **Pavillon Maurouard**, a striking two-storey building partly hidden by trees, crowned by a clock and an elegant little cupola. It is now an exhibition centre, named after the gunpowder engineer who designed the factory in 1873. It once housed three steam machines and four boilers, pre-dating 'Le Boris', which was added when the factory was extended. It is well worth going inside if it is open to see the beautiful iron corkscrew staircase leading to the second floor. There are only storerooms up there but I was delighted to be allowed to climb the narrow twisting stairs. The display I saw there, clearly aimed at children, showed how to identify wildlife by its traces and I found it fascinating. I

Pavillon Maurouard

can now identify the footprints and droppings of a weasel, a fox and lynx, should I ever chance to come across them. A useful free **map** of the park is available at the desk.

From the Pavillon entrance take the short path to the right which crosses the main path opposite and leads to a hidden pond, the **Mare au Martin-Pêcheur**, where I have occasionally seen mandarin ducks. With your back to the pond turn right and continue along the main path to a little grassy glade a few steps away, where the entrance to an inconspicuous woodland path is marked by a sign telling you that the towering tree overhead is a giant **sequoia**, a redwood tree native to California which can live for up to 3,500 years. Follow the winding little path to the left past two more sequoias, hidden in a little wood of their own. The path will lead you back to the main path which you left to visit the Pavillon.

Turn right and continue past the Mare au Martin-Pêcheur on the right and the **Musée des Poudres** on the left, in a building formerly used to store saltpetre. The display (in French) is fascinating but doesn't follow any obvious chronological order.

Continue along the path, following the worn rail lines

and take the first right after the Museum, a winding little woodland path with a yellow PR sign (see pp. 177-178) which goes past strange tree-covered mounds, called *merlons.* They were constructed to contain damage in case of an accidental explosion. There were several, the most serious being in 1937 when seven people were killed.

To the left of this PR path you can see the main path, which leads to the **Porte de Sevran** exit. But if you stick to the continuation of the woodland path you will see that you are circling the back of the Pavillon Maurouard, visible at the intersections of the path on the right. The path passes the **Mare en Croissant** on the left, a quiet algae-covered pond where I saw a moorhen swimming back to resume sitting on her eggs, clearly visible in a nest safely isolated in the middle of the water.

Continue past an abandoned factory building (no. 35) on the left to a larger pond with an islet in the middle, the **Mare à l'Ilot**, further along on the left. The islet is a favoured roosting

Mare à l'Ilot

place for birds. From here turn left and then first right to follow a paved PR path past three more arches, a building called 'Groupe XI' and the 'Boulodrome' before reaching the Boris and the remaining arches. After the last arch turn left to rejoin the main cycle path and follow the sign for 'Gare du Vert-Galant' back to the entrance at the Porte du Vert-Galant. Ignore the sign for 'Gare du Vert-Galant' to the right of the gate which is for cyclists, and continue downhill, back the way you came. The **RER station at Vert-Galant** is on the other side of the canal footbridge.

Optional 3 km canal walk to Villeparisis station

Turn right to continue along the towpath. There are slightly more people using this stretch of the canal but it is still quiet and mainly populated by ducks. I saw more violets and a clump of marsh marigolds growing by the water's edge. Eventually, after passing two more bridges you will come to the Pont de Mitry. Leave the towpath here and cross the bridge for the **RER station of Villeparisis Mitry-le-Neuf**.

If you feel like a drink before catching the train, turn right from the towpath for the small town centre of Villeparisis, but be warned that there is a dearth of cafés with tables outside here. With some misgivings, we finally approached a café called 'Le Marché', diagonally to the right across the small main square, where three men were sitting on chairs outside and asked the owner if we could bring out more chairs. His response was simply to tell the men in Turkish to give up their seats to us, which to our amazement they did, very graciously. Strangers, Anglophones, and women at that, were clearly a most unusual occurrence in this neighbourhood café, meriting special treatment. The café now has tables as well as chairs outside.

Distance from Paris: 18 km
(11 miles)
Depart: Gare du Nord
Arrive: Sevran-Livry
Journey time: 21 minutes
Length of visit: Half or full day
Alternative return from: Vert-Galant (Zone 4) or Villeparisis Mitry-le-Neuf (Zone 5)
Navigo Zone: 4
Single ticket: 4.95€ (5€ from Villeparisis)
Distance from Sevran-Livry station to Vert-Galant station: 2 km (1.2 miles)
Distance from Vert-Galant station to Villeparisis Mitry-le-Neuf station: 3 km (2 miles)
Population of Sevran: 51,225

Getting there

RER B trains to Mitry Claye, stopping at Sevran-Livry, run from the Gare du Nord every 15 minutes, returning at the same frequency up to midnight. The return journey from Villeparisis Mitry-le-Neuf takes 28 minutes.

Car: RN3, exit Vaujours centre.

RATP map *plan de secteur, no. 9*. See p. 179.

When to go

A mild sunny day at any time of the year is best for this outdoor visit. It is also suitable for a really hot day in summer, as the park and the towpath are mainly shady. In spring the canal and the park are full of wild flowers rarely seen so close to Paris. Go on a Sunday in spring, early summer or autumn if you want to visit the museum. If you go on a weekend during July or August you could combine a visit to the park with a kayak or canoe session on the Canal de l'Ourcq. See below.

Useful information

Parc de la Poudrerie, allée Eugène Burlot, 93410 Vaujours, tel 01 71 29 22 70, http://uk.tourisme93.com/parc-de-la-poudrerie.html in English. Open daily throughout the year.

Musée des Poudres in the park, tel 01 48 60 28 58. Open 2.30–5.30 pm on Sundays from March to June and from September to December, admission free. NB: closed in July and August. http://uk.tourisme93.com/poudrerie.html in English.

Pavillon Maurouard in the park, temporary exhibitions from 2-6 pm at weekends, admission free. Exhibition programme in French: http://www.tourisme93.com/document.php?pagendx=119.

Ourcq Can'ohe Club Sevranais, 31 boulevard de la République, Sevran 93270, tel 06 30 79 18 66 or 06 17 45 81 39, https://occs.clubeo.com. Open to the public during weekends in July and August from 10.30 am to 5 pm. 10€ for around 1½ hours, 5€ for under 16s. Equipment and instruction provided, no need to book. Beginners welcome but must be able to swim.

When you cross the canal bridge at Sevran turn right, instead of left for the park. The club is half a kilometre along the tow-path near a bridge. It is run under the auspices of the local authority and I have found it a well-run and welcoming place.

Cafés

It is a good idea to take a picnic to eat at the *buvette* in the park, which sells ice cream, soft drinks, tea and coffee at very modest prices.

Café Le Marché, 7 place du Marché, 77270 Villeparisis. Open daily.

2. Lagny-sur-Marne

A lively medieval market town with some surprising discoveries and a walk along the River Marne to the outdoor sculptures created by a local artist

Lagny doesn't get a star in the Michelin guide, as its glory days were over by the 14th century. Part of the rich county of Champagne in the Middle Ages, its great annual fair, second only to those of Provins and Troyes, once attracted merchant traders from as far afield as Flanders. But today, although it has an attractive riverside setting which inspired the neo-Impressionist Lagny group of painters at the turn of the 20th century, as well as a thriving market and an impressive abbey church, both dating from the early Middle Ages, it is not a centre for tourism. Its riches are concealed beneath a refreshingly modest exterior and you are likely to be the only foreign visitor. Lagny is on the fringe of the new town of Marne-la-Vallée but has kept its character as an agricultural market town, with a steadily growing population. It is particularly lively on market days.

You could limit your visit just to Lagny, but the contrast between the lively little town with its strong sense of continuity, the peaceful riverside walk to the slightly kitsch but impressive stone sculptures at the water's edge and then the bus ride to one of the new RER stations on the line to Disneyland will give you a rewarding glimpse into the small town life of the Île de France rarely seen by foreign visitors. And if you want a longer country walk you can cross the river at the new footbridge beside the statues and return to the station along the towpath on the other side.

Saint Fursy

Lagny's name comes from Latinius, the owner of a Roman villa on the banks of the Marne in the fourth century. A medieval town eventually took shape around the abbey founded there by an Irish Benedictine monk, St Fursy, around 650. The abbey was destroyed in the Viking raids of the ninth century, re-built in the 11th century and subsequently modified before being sold off in the Revolution, becoming first a military hospital and then part of the present Hôtel de Ville. The walled town with five gateways and eleven defensive towers reached the height of its prosperity in the 12th and 13th centuries, when the abbey church was built. No one knows why it was never completed to the original grand plan, but probably it was because the absorption of Champagne into the kingdom of France by a royal marriage in 1284 led to a decline in the region's importance and prosperity.

Suggested visit to Lagny-sur-Marne

The **station** is on the Thorigny side of the River Marne. Take the escalator up from the Paris platform, turn left and left again, down interior steps to the bus station exit. Go straight ahead along the rue du Maréchal Foch leading to Lagny on the other side of the bridge over the Marne. There is a little *café-tabac* on the corner, 'Les Terrasses', open on Sundays, with the best view of the river.

Continue over the bridge into Lagny, past the **tourist office** on your right, along the main street, rue du Chemin-de-Fer, which becomes the rue des Marchés leading to the **market** in the place de la Fontaine, the heart of the town. The fountain is a 1902 replacement of the original which marked the spot where the town's founder, St Fursy, is said to have struck a rock with his staff, revealing the waters of an underground spring. Markets and fairs have been held on this spot for nine centuries and its animated atmosphere on market days has a timeless quality. I photographed a pensive young woman dressed in black in a

Woman at a window overlooking the place de la Fontaine

long white apron with her hair in a bun at a window with blue shutters, looking like a detail from a 19th-century painting. On closer inspection of the photograph I saw that she was probably a waitress who had come to the window to smoke a cigarette.

As you enter the market place from the rue des Marchés, on your left you will see a massive 13th-century archway called **Passage de l'Arcade**, formerly a fortified entrance in the ramparts, leading to the Abbey and closed by a wooden portcullis (see p. 39). On market days the stalls almost block the entrance to this archway, which has a Revolutionary inscription in faded letters at the top, dated 1793:

UNITÉ

INDIVISIBILITÉ

DE LA RÉPUBLIQUE

LIBERTÉ

ÉGALITÉ FRATERNITÉ

OU LA MORT

Go through the archway and turn left to come to the **Cour**

Place de la Fontaine and Passage de l'Arcade

de l'Abbaye, a quiet little square far removed from the bustle of the market only a few feet away. It used to house the stables for the abbey and on the wall of one of the houses there is a sundial which reads *Sic vita fugit*—Thus life flees away.

Go back to the little street you came from and follow it in the other direction, past the back entrance of the **Hôtel de Ville**, built in 1755. If it is closed, you can peep through the glass door to glimpse its beautiful interior garden. It was the 18th-century cloister of the abbey and is surmounted by galleries in which, when it is open, you can see pictures by the Lagny group of painters.

The end of the street will bring you out into the surprisingly grand place de l'Hôtel de Ville which is dominated by the massive abbey church at the top, **Notre Dame des Ardents**. A commemorative plaque dated 1930 outside the front entrance to the Hôtel de Ville on the left recalls the visit of Joan of Arc to Lagny in 1430, en route from the coronation of Charles VII in Reims to her last battle in Compiègne, to stiffen the resolve of the inhabitants in fighting the English. It seems to have worked: in 1432 they made a brave sortie from the Porte Vacheresse in the ramparts to the south of the town and succeeded in lifting the siege led by the Duke of Bedford.

The church is named after the chapel of Notre Dame des Ardents, behind the altar, in memory of the successful prayers of the population in 1126 for the dreadful epidemic, 'le mal des ardents' (ergotism) to be lifted. This terrifying disease, in which the victim's limbs are attacked by gangrene, is now known to have been caused by the toxic effects of a fungus found in grain. In 1430 the church was the scene of an intervention by Joan of Arc, whose prayers temporarily revived a child who had been 'dead' of the disease for three days, allowing him to be baptised and buried in holy ground. She disclaimed later attempts to have it declared a miracle. The church itself mainly dates from 1205 but only the beautiful soaring chancel was completed to the original plan, which would have extended the length of the building to the place de la Fontaine. However, enough remains to give the visitor an uplifting sense of the power and elegant simplicity of the design.

Leaving the church by the main entrance, continue straight ahead to the place de la Fontaine. My favourite brasserie in the square is the **Saint Furcy** on the right (I have faithfully reproduced local variations in the spelling), patronised by the locals and the market-traders, with a terrace from where you have the best view of the action. That was before I discovered that its name is no accident: the interior was actually the nave of the 13th-century Église Saint Fursy, only the main entrance of which has survived. Make sure that you stop here at least for a drink so that you can visit *les toilettes.* There you will see the stone columns of the nave, concealed by the art-deco theme of the rest of the café, and an astonishing **stone bas-relief** of 'St Furci' himself, named in uneven but clear lettering, just inside the entrance to the lavatories. It looks earlier than the 13th century and may well pre-date the church, which was built on the remains of an older one. The stone washbasin with its automated brass tap appears to be the original *lavabo* used by the priest (see p. 28).

If you turn right from the Brasserie Saint Furcy and go a few steps down the rue St-Furcy, turning first right into the rue du Temple, you will see the sculpted Renaissance façade of the main doorway to the **Eglise St Fursy** which was demolished after the Revolution.

It is worth continuing along the rue du Temple to turn left into the rue St-Paul, where towards the end of the street on the left you will see the clear water of the **Lavoir de la Planchette**, set back from the road and protected by railings. It is fed by the same bubbling little spring which emerges at the Fontaine in the market place. It was a favourite meeting place for women doing the family wash in the 19th century, so much so that a local by-law was passed to restrict them from making too much noise. The social function of the *lavoir* as a clearing house for gossip was so well established that in some parts of France it was known as 'Radio Lavoir'.

Return to the place de la Fontaine. Facing you, right next to the passage de l'Arcade is the oldest house in Lagny, a former market hall called Les Cinq Pignons ('The Five Gables') whose 12th-century arcades housed the Flemish merchant-traders who came for the great annual fair. One of these arcades currently houses **Thé Art Café** (sic). Inside, a narrow winding medieval stone staircase leads, yet again, to *les toilettes.* The inhabitants of Lagny have a severely practical attitude to their history. If you go up the stairs at the back of the café on the ground floor and peep through the glass door, you will see a wonderful **medieval wooden staircase** curving around the thick beamed walls, which now leads to privately owned flats. There is a plaque outside the café to Léo Gausson (1860-1944), one of the Lagny group of painters, but no mention of its glorious medieval past.

Retrace your steps to the River Marne. Close to the bridge, at the corner of the rue du Chemin-de-Fer and the rue des Vieux-Moulins is the **Go Gorilla** restaurant with tables outside over-looking the river and a heated terrace in the rue du Chemin-de-Fer. Its bland modern decor looks deeply unpromising, but the young staff and the smokers at the terrace outside were friendly and the menu revealed it to be an obviously successful mix of traditional French dishes and fashionable cocktails, snacks and vegetarian options. I have yet to try it, but it is probably your best bet for food in Lagny. There is more seating upstairs with a good view of the river.

To the right of the restaurant you will see the round stone base of La Tour des Pêcheurs, the best-preserved remnant of Lagny's medieval defensive towers. At this point you could return over the bridge to the **station** or continue along the river to the sculptures, taking the bus at Montévrain to return to Paris via the station at Lagny Thorigny or the RER stations at Marne-la-Vallée–Chessy or Val d'Europe. There is also the option of crossing the river at the sculptures and returning to the station at Lagny-Thorigny along the towpath on the other side.

Optional 4 km walk to the Jardin des Sculptures de la Dhuys

Continue along the towpath, past a children's playground, some attractive 19th-century villas and a prettily located but rather chi-chi restaurant with a garden, La Villa, which might be worth a visit in summer. The views over the Marne are rewarding, with the sight and sounds of waterfowl, and the path soon

The towpath at Lagny-sur-Marne

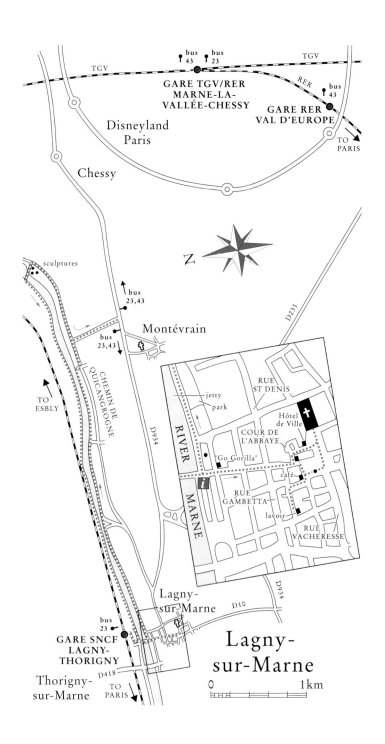

bus 43

bus 23

TGV

TGV

GARE TGV/RER
MARNE-LA-
VALLÉE-CHESSY

RER

bus 43

GARE RER
VAL D'EUROPE

Disneyland
Paris

TO
PARIS

Chessy

sculptures

Z

bus
23,43

Montévrain

bus
23,43

CHEMIN DE QUICANGROGNE

TO
ESBLY

D231

RUE
ST DENIS

jetty
park

Hôtel
de Ville

COUR DE
L'ABBAYE

RIVER

D934

'Go Gorilla'

café

i

RUE
GAMBETTA

MARNE

lavoir

RUE
VACHERESSE

D934

Lagny-
sur-Marne

D10

bus 23

GARE SNCF
LAGNY-
THORIGNY

D418

TO
PARIS

Lagny-
sur-Marne

Thorigny-
sur-Marne

0   1km

becomes muddy and more rustic, dotted with violets, cowslips and celandines in spring. After about a kilometre the GR sign (see pp. 177-178) will point you to the right to join the parallel country road, but we persisted with the narrow towpath for another kilometre, until it ran out and we had to join the road, the chemin de Quincangrogne, at the junction of a road leading uphill to Montévrain.

Turn left and continue to the **Moulin de Quincangrogne**, a former mill and then a paper factory, supposed to have originated as a hunting lodge for Henri IV, and now owned by the RATP, the Paris public transport authority. The name comes from a popular medieval expression, *Qui qu'en grogne*, which means roughly, 'Let them complain'.

Continue along the road and then the riverside path for another kilometre, keeping your eyes peeled for massed drifts of snowdrops if you come here in February.

The stone **sculptures** in the Parc des Statues will suddenly come into view, isolated or in groups, in a grassy field spreading from the road to the river, and quite bizarre they look. They are the work of a local sculptor, Jacques Servières, who since 1987 has been using the stones of the abandoned aqueduct bridge of the River Dhuis, which crossed the Marne here and was destroyed during the Second World War, to create monumental fantastic statues. His work is now supported by the local council. The statues are mainly of women and fabulous beasts and were originally inspired by the ones at Angkor Wat, but have changed with the development of the artist. He adds about two new statues each year. They have the appeal of the unexpected and, unlike nearby Disneyland, there are usually only a few people around to interrupt the view.

Optional 1½ km walk from the sculptures to the bus stops at Montévrain

From the sculptures return along the path you came by and take the road on the left just before the Moulin de Quincangrogne, the chemin de la Fontaine au Roi, which leads steeply uphill to the main road, the D934. The **Fontaine au Roi bus stop** for the 23 to Lagny-Thorigny SNCF station and the 43 to the RER station Val d'Europe is on your right, and the one on the other side of the road to the left is for the same buses in the other direction to the RER terminus at Marne-la-Vallée–Chessy, the stop for Disneyland. All three bus journeys take about 15 minutes to their terminus at the station. RER trains to Paris run more frequently than the SNCF trains from Lagny but take longer. Consult the timetables at the bus stops to decide which bus stop to wait at or use the Citymapper app. You will not have to wait more than half an hour for a bus in one direction or the other, even on a Sunday in winter.

I once took the 43 bus to Val d'Europe station because it came first. The journey through the misty flat Brie landscape, from where the new square boxes – factories, shopping malls and apartment blocks – loomed up, all looking identical, was a horrible eye-opener. The station was built in 2001 to serve the new town of Marne-la-Vallée and all the surrounding buildings date from then, an instructive contrast to Lagny-sur-Marne. The bus ride to Chessy or Lagny is a rather more cheerful experience.

Optional 4½ km walk from the sculptures to Lagny-Thorigny station

Cross the new footbridge at the Parc des Statues and turn left along the towpath, following the river all the way back to the bridge at Lagny and the station in Thorigny. It is considerably tamer than the walk on the Lagny side, endowed with a few benches and boardwalks, but it is pretty and traffic-free. We made a slight detour to see the old church at Dampmart en route, which was closed, as was the Café de la Mairie on a Sunday. Dampmart has a tiny *mairie* and a little shop as well as a Logis de France restaurant, the Quincangrogne, overlooking the river.

Distance from Paris: 35 km (22 miles)
Depart: Gare de l'Est
Arrive: Lagny-Thorigny
Journey time: 23 minutes
Length of visit: Half or full day
Alternative return from: RER Val d'Europe or RER Marne-la-Vallée–Chessy
Navigo Zone: 5
Single ticket: 5€
Distance from Lagny to the Fontaine au Roi bus stop: 5½ km (3½ miles)
Distance from Lagny to the sculptures and back to the station via the Marne: 8½ km (5.2 miles)
Population: 21,488

Getting there

SNCF trains to Meaux stopping at Lagny-Thorigny leave Gare de l'Est (*Île de France*) every half hour. Return service is also half-hourly, up to midnight.

RER A4 trains from the terminus at Marne-la-Vallée–Chessy, stopping at Val d'Europe, take 41 minutes to Châtelet-Les Halles and run every 15 minutes up to midnight.

Bus 23 from Fontaine au Roi to the stations at Lagny or Marne-la-Vallée–Chessy (terminus) runs approximately every half hour on weekdays, hourly at weekends. Bus 43 from Fontaine au Roi to the RER stations at Val d'Europe or Marne-la-Vallée–Chessy (terminus) runs every 20 minutes on weekdays, every 35 minutes on

Sundays. You can use a Paris métro ticket on these buses or your Navigo.

Car: A4, then A104 and D418.

When to go

Mild sunny weather is preferable for this mainly outdoor visit. If possible, go on a Wednesday, Friday or Sunday morning, when the market is in full swing up to around 1 pm.

Useful information

Office de tourisme de Marne et Gondoire, 2 rue du Chemin-de-Fer, 77400 Lagny, tel 01 64 02 15 15, www.marneetgondoire-tourisme. fr. Closed Monday and Thursday. In summer open 9.30 am–1 pm and 2–5.30 pm, 4 pm on Sunday. Closes at 5 pm on weekdays in winter.

Parc des Statues de la Dhuys, www.jardindesculpture.net, website of the sculptor, Jacques Servières.

Restaurants

Le Saint Furcy café/brasserie, 6 place de la Fontaine, Lagny, tel 01 64 30 04 71. Open to 8 pm Tuesday to Saturday, and to around 1 pm on Sundays, when it does not serve food. The remains of the 13th century church concealed inside its *toilettes* make this friendly family-run café with its popular terrace overlooking the market place an experience not to be missed. The food is nothing special but it is traditional and honest and so are the prices.

Go Gorilla brasserie/restaurant, 3 rue du Chemin-de-Fer, Lagny, tel 01 60 31 95 38, www.go-gorilla.fr. Open daily to 11 pm. Menu at 25€, two-course menu 18€, *plat du jour* 14.50€ on weekdays, around 20€ at weekends.

50cl carafe of wine from 15€. It is probably a good idea to book on Sundays if you want a table upstairs, where there is the best view of the river.

La Villa, 111 quai de la Gourdine, Lagny, tel 01 64 02 37 18, www.lavilla-restaurant.fr. Open daily, weekday lunchtime menus 19.80€ and 40.80€, weekends 40.80€, and *à la carte*.

3. Meaux

A visit to the medieval heart of Meaux and an optional walk along the rural Canal de Chalifert to Esbly

I found this lovely walk, along an isolated spit of land between the River Marne and the Canal de Chalifert, by studying the map, looking for somewhere rural and little-known but within easy reach of Paris. It led to the discovery of the astonishingly well-preserved medieval centre of Meaux clustered around its imposing cathedral with its hidden bishop's garden, bishop's palace and chapter house, and of the historic bridge leading to the medieval market quarter and the little-frequented Canal de Chalifert. The optional 10 km walk along the canal is easy and varied: secluded and mysterious near Meaux, with wild flowers growing profusely along the towpath, followed by an optional detour to the village of Mareuil-lès-Meaux, and continuing past open fields and woodland, passing an old-fashioned hotel-restaurant with a beautiful view over the Marne. You are un-likely to meet more than one or two people on this walk until you reach the small town of Esbly and the station.

Bossuet, the eloquent bishop of Meaux

Situated in a kind of natural amphitheatre at a bend in the Marne and at the confluence of road and river routes in the flat Brie countryside, Meaux was the capital of a Celtic tribe, from which its name derives, before it became a Roman town. It has been a bishopric since the fourth century and was one of the capitals of Brie under the Counts of Champagne. It has always been an important religious and commercial centre, its fortunes closely linked to those of nearby Paris. Its most famous bishop was Jacques-Bénigne Bossuet (1627-1704), preacher to the court of

Meaux Cathedral overlooking the Marne

Louis XIV and tutor to the Dauphin, renowned for the power of his oratory.

Today Meaux is a centre for local industry and has several colleges, lycées and a university. Its dynamic right-wing mayor, Jean-François Copé, has encouraged the destruction of the tower blocks of the 1960s in favour of a mix of private and low-level social housing. Gastronomically, it is celebrated for the local Brie de Meaux cheese and the Moutarde de Meaux which includes mustard seeds, originally made to a secret recipe for the bishops of Meaux. To most Parisians it is merely a large town close to Paris, so I was agreeably surprised to discover its compact medieval centre. It is practically unknown to foreign visitors.

Suggested visit to Meaux

Take the exit 'place de la Gare' and turn left from the station, past the car park on the left. Cross the main road at the pedestrian crossing, towards the cathedral which you can see in front of you and continue past the Lycée Henri Moissan, where the writer Michel Houellebecq was a pupil. Go past the 19th-century Hotel de Ville on your right and turn left into the place d'Henri Moissan and along the little rue de Martimprey, which leads straight to the **cathedral**.

Built between the 12th and 16th centuries, this contains every variation of Gothic but the total impression is one of harmony. The sheer power of the Church in the Middle Ages is reflected in the soaring nave, filled with slanting light. To the right and left of the entrance are two large sculptures of Bossuet, one of him seated, the other of him preaching. To the right of the carpeted choir I once saw a small typed notice reproducing the epitaph on his tomb, with a neatly handwritten explanatory footnote: 'La tombe de Bossuet est sous le tapis' ('The tomb of Bossuet is under the carpet'). When I last visited the carpet had been removed, along with the notice.

On leaving the cathedral, to the right you will see an arched entrance framing **Le Jardin de Bossuet**, visible through another, larger archway. The **office de tourisme** is on the left, just before the entrance to the garden and *les toilettes*. Spare a glance to the right for the harmonious ensemble formed by the medieval chapter house and the bishop's palace housing the **Musée Bossuet**, worth a visit if you are not doing the walk to Esbly, and go through the arch into the tranquil walled garden, which

Meaux Cathedral, entrance to Jardin de Bossuet

was laid out by Le Nôtre in the form of a bishop's mitre in 1642. The wall at the end was once part of the Gallo-Roman ramparts. Bossuet loved to work in this garden, which is full of flowers and restful walks. There is a deliciously scented mauve tea rose named after him, with a notice drawing your attention to it, in front of you just to the right of the entrance.

The little medieval streets around the cathedral are lively, with café tables in front of the church in summer and a variety of restaurants. However, almost everything is closed on Sunday, apart from several fast food outlets. An exception is the recently opened **La Maison Meldoise**, a little way down the rue St-Rémy in front of the cathedral, on the left. The menu features regional specialities such as Brie de Meaux as well as traditional dishes and the inevitable burgers, and they sell little pots of Meaux mustard. It was full of local families when I tried it one Sunday and the décor is cosy, but I have to say that I found the dish I ordered, a 'briflette' consisting mainly of potatoes and melted Brie cheese with a minuscule sprinkling of lardons and onions, rather over-priced at 15.50€.

It might be worth trying the brasserie-restaurant **Le Cirkus,** also newly opened, a few steps further on towards the river. Turn right from La Meldoise into the little rue des Vieux-Moulins, cross the road ahead and you will see Le Cirkus in front of you, with the Hotel de Ville on your left. The décor is restful and there are two terraces, enclosed and heated in winter. The owners have made an effort to cater for varying needs, with cheese and charcuterie platters and vegetarian options as well as more traditional dishes. I have only had coffee here, at lunchtime on a rainy Sunday, and was given a warm welcome. It seems just as popular with local families as La Meldoise.

You could return to the **station** from here, but I strongly recommend discovering the historic quarter known as 'Le Marché' on the other side of the Marne. You could return to the station by crossing the Marne by another bridge (see below) or continue on the little-known walk along the Canal de Chalifert to the next station at Esbly.

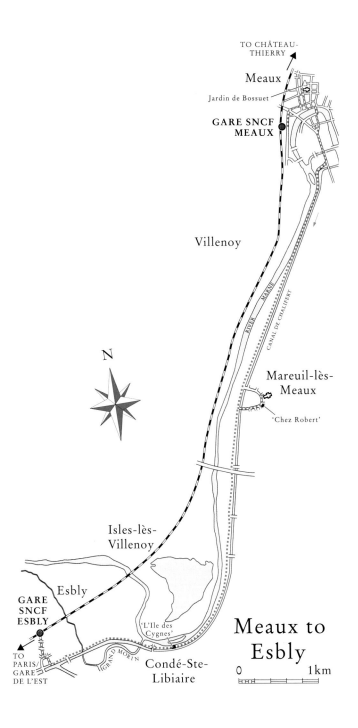

TO CHÂTEAU-
THIERRY

Meaux

Jardin de Bossuet

**GARE SNCF
MEAUX**

Villenoy

RIVER MARNE

CANAL DE CHALIFERT

Mareuil-lès-
Meaux

'Chez Robert'

Isles-lès-
Villenoy

Esbly

**GARE
SNCF
ESBLY**

'L'Ile des
Cygnes'

TO
PARIS/
GARE
DE L'EST

GRAND MORIN

Condé-Ste-
Libiaire

N

Meaux to
Esbly

0   1km

Optional 10 km walk along the Canal de Chalifert to Esbly

Keeping the Hotel de Ville on your left, cross the main road towards the river, with a bridge on each side of the pedestrian crossing. Turn left and continue across the **Pont du Marché**, a beautiful bridge with several arches spanning the Marne. From what I have been able to discover it dates from 1540 but was preceded by earlier versions and has been rebuilt several times since. For centuries it was the only bridge at Meaux. Heavily fortified, it marked the physical division and historic tension between the aristocratic ecclesiastical 'Ville' and the commercially important 'Marché', the breadbasket of Paris. During the 'Jacquerie', the popular uprising of 1358, it was the scene of a massacre in which the bodies of hundreds of peasants were flung into the river.

After the bridge you will pass the covered **market** on your right, built in 1879, on a spot where local produce, especially cheese, has been sold for centuries. To return to the **station** from here turn right at the place du Marché and continue straight on along the rue Jean Bureau which leads to the other bridge, with the station opposite on the left.

To find the Canal de Chalifert, continue straight on when the road joins the rue Cornillon. On your left you will pass Pizza Time, where for 4.50€ I had one of the best slices of pizza I have ever eaten. Carry straight on until you see a canal bridge ahead and a shop called 'Antiquités Meaux' on the left. Cross the road at the pedestrian crossing here and continue over the bridge, which spans the medieval Canal de Cornillon. Take the first street on the right after the bus stop, the rue Terfaux and then turn left into the rue St-Rigomer. Follow it to the end and continue along the towpath beside the **Canal de Chalifert**.

From here the walk is straightforward, with wild flowers almost smothering the narrow winding path, margeurites, dog roses, harebells, poppies, buddleia and wild mint in summer, violets and buttercups in spring. I have only ever met one or two other walkers and the silence is hardly disturbed by the occasional huge barge sliding past or a noisy duck. You could picnic or sunbathe here in the middle of the path as no one is likely to step on you.

After less than 2 km the first bridge you see leads to the centre of the small village of **Mareuil-lès-Meaux**. This decaying bridge is now closed off, but you can take the second bridge a little further on, turning left after crossing it to reach the village centre. It is worth the detour for its 11th-century **church** in a peaceful tree-lined little square with a sunny bench. Sadly, the owner of **Chez Robert**, its one *café/tabac*/restaurant and the centre of village life, will have retired by the time you read this, but I hope the café will still be in existence under a new owner.

The church is a little further on. Although it is usually locked there are two interesting plaques beside the entrance. The one on the left says that Pierre Ronsard, 'The Prince of Poets', was the *curé commandataire* here, 1552-1554. The one on the right, put up by the Canadian government, commemorates Émile Petitot, 1838-1916, scholar and missionary in the Northwest Territories of Canada, who spent the last 30 years of his life as *curé* of this church.

Return to the bridge and turn left back onto the towpath which is wider at this point, lending itself to a brisker pace. I have seen snowdrops growing to the right of the path here in early March. Continue for another 3 km, with fields on your right, past a blue bridge with a new *autoroute* soaring overhead just beyond it. You will pass another bridge with a small road leading to it. Do not cross it but continue to follow the canal. Eventually the woodland on your right gives way to large rambling back gardens belonging to houses which front the Marne, hidden on the other side. Continue until you have almost reached another bridge ahead.

Just before it, one of the houses has the word 'Restaurant' in fading red capitals painted on it, almost obscured by foliage. This is the back garden of the **Île des Cygnes** hotel, the front of which has a sunny terrace overlooking the Île des Cygnes (Swan Island) on the Marne and a small clientèle, mainly long-term residents of the hotel. The barman introduced us to a young mallard duck happily splashing about in a plastic bath in the garden. He had reared it from a duckling and taught it to defend itself from the cat, which was watching it with wary interest. Try the back entrance to the hotel, and if it is closed continue to the bridge. If it is open, the front terrace with its lovely view over the river is an idyllic spot in which to sit and watch the swans over a drink. From the front entrance turn left to continue along the little road beside the Marne, turning first left to find the bridge.

Do not cross the bridge but continue along the Quai du Canal which soon crosses the Marne at its confluence with the Grand Morin on your right. The two rivers flow under the Canal de Chalifert, which at this point is actually a bridge. Continue along the canal, which is still rural but with a few more people in evidence. You will pass the confluence of a tributary of the Grand Morin with the canal, a favourite place for fishermen, just before another bridge. Do not cross it, but continue along the towpath until you see a road bridge ahead, which means you are in Esbly.

Take the first road on the right before the bridge, next to the sign 'Quai du Canal', with a little green to the left. Turn left at the end and cross the busy road in front of you at the pedestrian crossing. Follow the main street, the rue du Général Leclerc facing you, through the little town of Esbly right to the end. There are several cafés, but the only one open on Sunday is opposite the **station**, which you will find facing you at the end of the road, on the left. The trains for Paris leave from the platform in front of you.

Distance from Paris: 45 km (28 miles)
Depart: Gare de l'Est
Arrive: Meaux
Journey time: 25 or 39 minutes
Length of visit: Half or full day
Alternative return from: Esbly
Navigo Zone: 5
Single ticket: 5€
Distance from Meaux to Esbly: 10 km (6 miles)
Population: 53,766 (Meaux); 6,189 (Esbly)

Getting there

Fast SNCF trains to Château-Thierry leave hourly from Gare de l'Est (*Île de France*) stopping at Meaux 25 minutes later. Slower trains to Meaux run twice an hour, taking 39 minutes. Return service is up to midnight, at the same frequency. Return trains from Esbly run three times an hour, taking 30 or 36 minutes.
Car: A4 or RN3, exit Meaux.

When to go

Mild sunny weather is preferable for this long walk, which is at its prettiest in spring and summer, but you could visit Meaux at any time of the year as the cathedral is always open, except at lunchtime. Bossuet's garden is always open. The Musée Bossuet is closed on Tuesday. The market is held on Saturday morning up to 1 pm.

Useful information

Office de tourisme, 1 place Paul Doumer, 77100 Meaux, tel 01 64 33 02 26, www.tourisme-paysde meaux.fr. Open daily in summer 9.30 am–12.30 pm and 2–6 pm. Open in winter Tuesday-Saturday 9.30 am–12.30 pm and 2–5 pm, and 2–5 pm on Sundays.

The **Cathedral** is open at the same times as the tourist office. The **Jardin de Bossuet** is open daily.

Musée Bossuet in the former Bishop's Palace, 5 place Charles de Gaulle, Meaux, tel 01 64 34 84 45, www.musee-bossuet.fr. Open at the same times as the tourist office, except Tuesdays when it is closed all day. Admission 4€, concessions 3€. Free to everyone on the first Sunday of the month.

Cafés and restaurants

La Maison Meldoise, 33 rue Saint-Rémy, Meaux, tel 01 60 23 43 63, www.lamaisonmeldoise.fr. Open for lunch Thursday-Sunday. Three-course menu 26€ or à la carte, 50 cl *pichet* of wine 9.25€.

Le Cirkus brasserie/restaurant, 9 place de l'Hotel de Ville, Meaux, tel 01 64 35 75 42, www. le-cirkus.fr. Open daily. Main dishes such as *souris d'agneau* (roast knuckle of lamb) 23€, risotto 16€, *planche mixte* (platter of cheese and charcuterie to share) 21€, 50 cl *pichet* of wine from 15€.

L'Île des Cygnes, hotel-restaurant-café, 12 bis quai de la Marne, 77450 Condé Sainte Libiaire, tel 01 64 63 54 73. Unpredictable opening hours. Paris prices in the restaurant. Technically closed in the afternoon, but they opened up for us when we tapped on the back window.

4. La Ferté-sous-Jouarre

An old town on the River Marne, once 'the millstone
capital of the world', and a country walk to the striking
early Christian tombs in the crypts at Jouarre

La Ferté-sous-Jouarre (*ferté* means 'stronghold') seems just another picturesque old town on a river at first glance. No trace remains of its tenth-century fortress, constructed on an island near
the right bank of the River Marne at its confluence with a smaller
river, Le Petit Morin, and there are few visible reminders of its
prosperous manufacturing past. But it is the nearest station for
the tiny hilltop town of Jouarre, reached by a pretty 3 km country walk or by taxi, whose Benedictine abbey was founded in the
seventh century. The crypts contain the intriguingly decorated
tombs of the abbey's founders, the best-preserved tombs of this
period in Western Europe, and are the high point of the visit.

Although La Ferté-sous-Jouarre seems to be clearly in decline, it is an engaging little market town and its outskirts might
be well worth exploring on a separate trip. Its abandoned quar-
ries are in two woods behind the station, the Bois de la Barre and
the Bois de la Bergette, both now protected as 'Espaces Naturels
Sensibles' (fragile green spaces). The Parc de la Fontaine aux
Pigeons on a hill above the town on the Jouarre side of the river
did not feel like a park at all, but more like a hidden forest. We
did not meet a soul there and were charmed by its air of mystery.
I have also followed the Marne out of town in both directions
and found the walks peaceful and rewarding.

Millstones and Merovingians

During the Middle Ages the siliceous stone quarried from the
banks of the Petit Morin at La Ferté-sous-Jouarre was used to

La Ferté-sous-Jouarre from the bridge

make millstones so reputed for their durability that by the 19th century they were being exported by river and then by train all over the world. In 1853 at the peak of production there were over 20 millstone companies in the town producing 20,000 millstones annually. But by the end of the 19th century automation was beginning to kill the demand and the last company manufacturing millstones at La Ferté-sous-Jouarre closed down in 1951.

The nearby hilltop town of Jouarre was a former Gallo-Roman settlement, chosen as the site of an abbey around 635 AD by St Adon during the reign of King Dagobert I, a member of the Merovingian dynasty that ruled the Franks from 481 to 751. The abbey became a pilgrimage site in the early Middle Ages, and a small fortified town took shape around it. The Abbaye Notre Dame, whose early abbesses came from some of the leading families of France, is still functioning.

Suggested visit to La Ferté-sous-Jouarre

Take the underpass for the main exit from the **station**, cross the road towards the Café de la Gare and continue parallel to

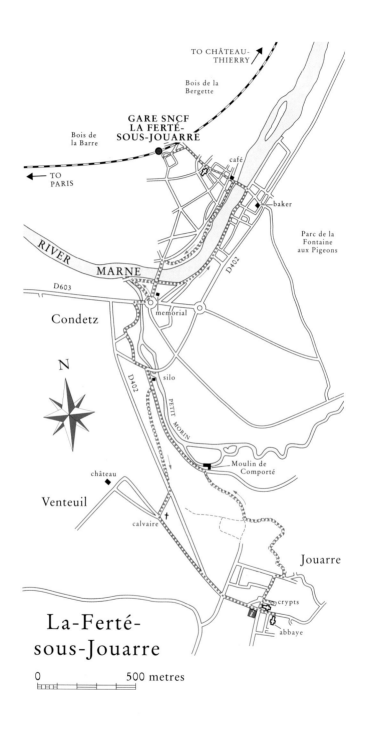

TO CHÂTEAU-
THIERRY

Bois de la
Bergette

**GARE SNCF
LA FERTÉ-
SOUS-JOUARRE**

Bois de
la Barre

café

TO
PARIS

baker

RIVER

MARNE

D402

Parc de la
Fontaine
aux Pigeons

D603

Condetz

memorial

N

D402

silo

PETIT MORIN

Moulin de
Comporté

château

Venteuil

calvaire

Jouarre

crypts

La-Ferté-
sous-Jouarre

abbaye

0   500 metres

the railway line, along the lower part of the street to the end. Halfway along, you will see a millstone set into the wall on your left, assembled from separate pieces *à l'anglaise,* as opposed to the older method of using one whole stone. It was the adoption of this English technique which contributed to the flourishing of millstone manufacture here in the 19th century.

At the end of the road turn right into the rue Michel Fauvet past some attractive large houses decorated with coloured tiles, a reminder of the town's former prosperity. It leads to the place de l'Hôtel de Ville, where there is a small **market** on Sundays, dominated by the striking neo-gothic Hôtel de Ville with its clock tower, dated 1885.

Continue straight on into the rue des Pelletiers. At a corner on the left just before the bridge is the friendly café **Chez Martine**, formerly Au Bon Coin, with a little terrace off the main street. Martine is very accommodating to clients who bring their own sandwiches as, like all the other cafés, she does not offer food on Sundays.

From the Carrefour City supermarket opposite, a useful source for picnic supplies which closes at 1 pm on Sundays, turn right into a little street, place Reguard de l'Île, which leads to a park beside the river. The riverside path is frequented by fishermen and from the walk above it is shaded with lime trees. Continue past the children's play area and turn right and then left to cross the bridge. On the other side on the left is a huge white **memorial** erected by the Royal Engineers to commemorate the 3,740 members of the British Expeditionary Force who lost their lives here fighting alongside the French in the Battle of the Marne in 1914, a battle that saved Paris and France from invasion.

3 km walk to Jouarre via the Château de Venteuil

From the memorial, cross the road to the right at the pedestrian crossing, continue around the roundabout and cross at another pedestrian crossing onto the D603, signposted 'Jouarre'. Turn right, continue over a little bridge across the Petit Morin river and take the second little road on the left, the rue du Petit Pays, marked with the red and white GR sign (see pp. 177–178). Continue along this quiet residential road which follows the Petit Morin for a little way, keeping to the left (the road forks twice) until you reach a huge silo half covered with foliage, next to a little lock and weir. Go past the 'Billard Club Fertois' and the silo and follow the uphill GR footpath on the right, through woodland.

The footpath eventually comes out onto the D402. Turn left and cross the road to take the first road on the right, signposted 'Venteuil ferme et château, 0.5 km'. Continue uphill until you reach a *calvaire* (roadside cross) on your left. The road to the right leads to the invisible and privately-owned Château de Venteuil, built in 1760. It was Napoleon's headquarters in 1814 and it was from a bench where the *calvaire* now stands, with a view over the valleys of the Marne and the Petit Morin, that he watched his troops in an earlier Battle of the Marne, on the 2nd of March 1814.

Turn left, past the *calvaire*, and take the dead straight tree-lined little asphalt road. You will see the church spire of Jouarre ahead of you. The little road eventually joins the main road, signposted 'Jouarre centre ville'. Continue to the crossroads and turn right for the **tourist office**, opposite the Mairie in place Auguste Tinchant. There is a friendly PMU café, **Le Vincennes**, which closes around 2 pm on Sundays, next to the tourist office, and a pizza takeaway and kebab shop on either side of the Mairie.

The tourist office opposite the Mairie is an obligatory stop if you want to see the **crypts** and the atmospheric parish church, **Eglise de St Pierre et St Paul**, burned down by the English during the Hundred Years' War and rebuilt at the beginning of the 16th century. These can only be visited with a tourist office guide.

The **Abbaye Notre Dame de Jouarre** is to the right of the Mairie in the rue Montmorin. The tranquil atmosphere of this little street, full of roses in June, is that of a cathedral close, with an ancient porch at the end. The community of Benedictine nuns belongs to an institution which has functioned almost without a break since its foundation by St Adon. People still come here to make retreats. En route you will pass *les toilettes publiques* and a little terrace which belongs to the only restaurant in Jouarre, **Les Terrasses de la Crypte**. I had no idea of the existence of this fairly new restaurant so have not yet tried it but went inside on a rainy Sunday to ask for their card. The *patron* was friendly and the customers looked happy.

The striking 12th-century **Tour Romane** next door has been incorporated into the present abbey buildings and now houses a gift shop, run by the nuns. You can visit the nuns' atmospheric 18th-century church, next to the Tour Romane, from the entrance of which you can glimpse their enclosed garden.

The **Merovingian crypts** are to the right of the Eglise St Pierre et St Paul. They originally belonged to two separate churches and were joined together in the 17th century. A primitive sculpture of the prophet Elijah with a raven perched on his shoulder and a piece of bread in his hand is above the entrance, which once was at ground level but is now several steps down.

The more interesting crypt is to the left (see photograph p. 25). Its marble pillars came from the Roman Temple of Jupiter which stood on that site and from nearby fourth-century Roman villas. Their elegant capitals were sculpted in the seventh century, inspired by classical models. This crypt contains the empty sarcophagi of the founders of the Abbey, mostly belonging to the same family. The most immediately striking is that of St Agilbert (*c.* 673) with a unique bas-relief frieze of the Last Judgement showing people praying with uplifted hands, revealing the influence of Coptic Christians from Egypt.

The much later 13th-century tomb of the Irish princess St Ozanne is in the far corner, next to the simple tomb of St Adon. It is surmounted by a beautiful sculpture of her lying with a little dog at her feet, symbol of fidelity. I was told that it was the work of the sculptor who carved the famous figures of the kings and queens of France in the Basilique St-Denis.

The tomb of St Telchide, the first abbess (*c.* 750) is decorated with flowing, almost abstract patterns in the Celtic style, the fleur de lys, symbol of purity, and scallop shells, a symbol of light derived from the Roman habit of using these shells as oil lamps, as well as a reference to the Gospel parable of the Wise and Foolish Virgins: ten virgins were invited to a late night marriage feast and fell asleep waiting for the bridegroom (a symbolic reference to Christ); all had brought lamps but five

Jouarre crypt tombstone, Christ in Majesty

had brought oil for their lamps and five had not. While the foolish virgins were trying to buy oil, the bridegroom appeared and
the five wise virgins went in to the feast, but the foolish virgins
arrived too late and were turned away.

The tomb of St Agilbert nearby is decorated with swastikas,
recalling the motif's ancient significance as a symbol of light. The
cosmopolitan fusion of cultures and the assured craftsmanship
of the work are fascinating evidence of the continuity of the so-
called Dark Ages with the Roman world and beyond.

The most impressive sight of all comes at the end when the
guide unlocks a little door outside the crypt to reveal the hidden
end of the tomb of St Agilbert, concealed by the wall, which is
covered with another unique bas relief, Christ in Majesty surrounded by the symbols of the Four Evangelists. It looks as
fresh as the day it was carved, because of the limestone earth
which covered it and has preserved it down the centuries. Now
back-lit and protected by glass, it has been accessible to public
view for around 30 years. When I last visited Jouarre the tourist

office was closed and the crypts were locked, but the little door outside had been left open so that people could still stoop to go along the vaulted passage to view the bas relief, softly lit behind its glass case.

3 km walk from Jouarre to La Ferté-sous-Jouarre via the Petit Morin

On leaving the crypts, follow the PR path by turning right down the rue du Petit Palais to the end, then right into the rue de la Pierre and first left into the ruelle de la Prévode, a grassy path which curves to the right and continues downhill. At the very end of this path where it comes into a clearing with a **view** over the valley (see photograph p. 16) turn left, following the discreet blue PR left-turn sign painted on a tree. (The local PR signs here are blue, instead of the usual yellow.) Continue along the woodland path, which can be extremely muddy in winter.

When you reach a clearing in the wood where two paths meet, follow the PR sign right, fairly steeply downhill. The path comes out at an old millhouse, the Moulin de Comporté, on a quiet little road beside the Petit Morin. Turn left down this road, marked with an X, meaning that this is not the PR path, and you will eventually arrive back at the silo, on a parallel path to the one you started from.

Retrace your steps until you emerge from the rue du Petit Pays onto the D603. Turn right and go back over the pedestrian crossing at the roundabout. Behind the advertising billboard there is a white gravel path with a wooden bar across it to your left, which follows the right bank of the Petit Morin.

Follow this pretty and secluded GR path for a short way until you see a little bridge, beneath which the Petit Morin flows into the Marne. Continue under the bridge by the lower river-side footpath for a superb close-up **view** of the confluence of the two rivers and turn right to follow the Marne. Continue along the riverside footpath, under the road bridge you crossed on the way to Jouarre and past the British 1914 war memorial. Further along there are steps down to a curious narrow path, the

Promenade du Port aux Meules. It is lined with 500 millstones weighing between one and five tons piled up in layers to form a wall four metres high. It was built between 1860 and 1870 to allow millstones to be loaded even when the river was in flood. Above the end of the Promenade are the half-ruined remains of the millstone workshops.

Continue along the river until you come to a pretty iron road bridge bedecked with flowers in summer. It was enlarged in 1865 to facilitate the passage of the huge barges needed to transport the millstones and leads into the rue des Pelletiers. Go back the way you came to the **station**.

If you visit on a weekday you will find the Café de la Gare open. We received a warm welcome there, foreign visitors clearly being something of a novelty in these parts.

Distance from Paris: 55 km
Depart: Gare de l'Est
Arrive: La Ferté-sous-Jouarre
Journey time: 42 minutes
Length of visit: Full day
Navigo Zone: 5
Single ticket: 5€
Distance from La Ferté to Jouarre and back: 6 km (3.7 miles)
Population: 9,504 (La Ferté-sous-Jouarre); 4,190 (Jouarre)

Getting there

SNCF trains to Château-Thierry stopping at La Ferté-sous-Jouarre leave Gare de l'Est (*Île de France*) every hour, returning hourly up to around 11.30 pm.

Car: A4 from Porte de Bercy, then exit 18 for La Ferté-sous-Jouarre.

Taxi: from La Ferté-sous-Jouarre to Jouarre approximately 8€, tel 01 60 22 23 55, mobile 06 23 89 36 22.

When to go

Good weather is preferable for this mainly outdoor visit. The Merovingian crypts are closed on Monday and on Tuesday and Sunday in winter. The market is on Sunday, a day when the cafés do not serve food, not even a sandwich. See below for suggestions.

Useful information

Espace Jouarre Tourisme, 6 place Auguste Tinchant, 77640 Jouarre, tel 01 64 03 88 09, www.coulom mierspaysdebrie-tourisme.fr/ les-inattendus/les-cryptes-

merovingiennes-de-jouarre.
Open 9.30 am–1 pm and 2.30–6 pm
Wednesday to Saturday, on Tuesday afternoons and on Sunday
mornings in summer. In winter
open Wednesday–Saturday to
5 pm. You must buy tickets to visit
the crypts at the tourist office as
someone has to accompany you to
the crypts and unlock the door.
Admission 4€.

I strongly recommend ringing
before setting out, to make sure
the tourist office is open. If you
arrive when it is closed it is worth
asking at the Abbaye Notre Dame
if they could kindly let you in to
see the crypts.

Restaurants and cafés

If you go on a Sunday there is
nothing except fast food available
in La Ferté-sous-Jouarre, so I recommend taking a picnic, buying a
sandwich or trying out the new
restaurant in Jouarre. There is a
baker at the end of the rue du
Faubourg, on the the other side of
the bridge, who will make sandwiches to order.

Chez Martine café, 12 rue des
Pelletiers, La Ferté-sous-Jouarre,
tel 01 60 32 98 58. Closed on
Monday and closes on Sunday at 1
or 2 pm, depending on the demand.

**Les Terrasses de la Crypte
brasserie**, rue de la Tour, 77640
Jouarre, tel 06 82 21 49 32,
www.facebook.com/lesterrasses
jouarre. Open Wednesday to
Sunday and sells reasonably
priced salads, steaks and char-
cuterie/cheese platters.

Le Vincennes PMU café, 14
Grande Place, Jouarre. Open every day except Monday. Clientèle
of local men watching sport on
TV screens. Friendly ambiance.
The *patron* was more than happy
to serve us a glass of wine to accompany the sandwiches we had
brought.

5. Neuilly-sur-Marne

**An easy tranquil walk to a little-known *guinguette* on the
Marne and along the rural Canal de Chelles**

The modern commuter town of Neuilly-sur-Marne is so close
to Paris that you will be pleasantly surprised to find yourself enjoying a peaceful stroll along the river within minutes of getting
off the train. The *guinguette* (riverside restaurant where people
go to dance) is only a short distance from the station, but in
a different world. The nearby marina gives it a holiday atmosphere and unlike the better-known establishments near Joinville,
it is mainly patronised by locals.

 If you are pressed for time you could return to Paris
the way you came, but it is well worth prolonging the walk
along the surprisingly rural Canal de Chelles, where you will
meet only a few strollers. From there it is a short bus ride to the
station at Chelles-Gournay or you could walk the two kilometres to the station through a quiet residential quarter, peeping
into well-kept suburban gardens. There is a popular café with a
terrace in front of the station, with a relaxed, almost provincial
atmosphere.

Les guinguettes

Guinguettes (pronounced 'gang-ETTE') are traditional modestly-
priced restaurants by the river where people go to dance. One
theory is that they are so called because *le petit blanc*, the white
wine of the Paris region they served, made people *giguet* (ready
to dance a jig). Scores of open-air restaurants serving this wine
and its traditional accompaniment, *la petite friture* (tiny fried
fish, usually whitebait) opened along the banks of the Seine and
especially the Marne in the 19th century to avoid the tax on

Guinguette Chez Fifi

goods coming into the capital. Working Parisians would spend Sunday afternoons beside the river, eating, drinking and listening to popular songs played on the accordion, until they felt ready to get up and dance.

Attracting artists as well as artisans, the *guinguettes* recall the atmosphere of the inter-war years, evoked by the songs of Edith Piaf, the films of Marcel Carné and the novels of Georges Simenon, all of whom came under their spell. Although these days most of them are no longer particularly cheap, they are always cheerful and they have never entirely disappeared from the affection of Parisians, despite the lure of television which nearly killed them off in the 1960s. In fact, in the last 30 years or so there has been a revival of the tradition, with the long-established *guinguettes* at Joinville now featuring in the guidebooks and a newer one on an island at Champigny, the Île du Martin-

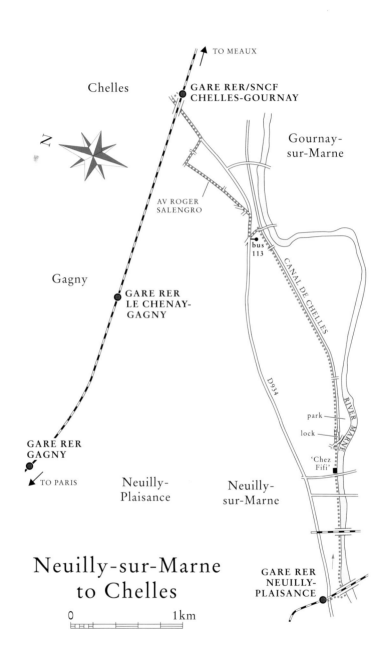

TO MEAUX

Chelles

GARE RER/SNCF
CHELLES-GOURNAY

Gournay-
sur-Marne

N

AV ROGER
SALENGRO

CANAL DE CHELLES

bus
113

Gagny

GARE RER
LE CHENAY-
GAGNY

D934

park

lock

GARE RER
GAGNY

'Chez
Fifi'

RIVER MARNE

TO PARIS

Neuilly-
Plaisance

Neuilly-
sur-Marne

GARE RER
NEUILLY-
PLAISANCE

Neuilly-sur-Marne
to Chelles

0   1km

Pêcheur, attracting a younger clientèle. Chez Fifi, described below, is resolutely anchored in the 1960s and 70s, and its prices are still modest.

4 km walk from Neuilly-Plaisance station to Pointe de Gournay bus stop

Leave the **station** via the exit marked 'Sortie 2, Boulevard Gallieni', go through the ticket barrier and walk down a further flight of steps. At the bottom of the steps ignore the walkway directly in front of you and turn round to the left until you are facing in the opposite direction. You will see a discreet red and white GR sign (see pp. 177-178) facing you, in the right hand corner of what appears to be a dead end, but isn't. Continue straight on, beneath the railway line overhead which crosses the river ahead of you. The walkway ends in steps down to the water's edge, where you are immediately in another world, with the quiet spacious river glittering in front of you.

Turn left and walk along the Marne for a kilometre, passing a few strollers and joggers and the occasional water-skier in summer, until you come to **Chez Fifi**, just after the fourth bridge. It has tables outside, a dance floor inside and accordion music with live bands at the weekends.

The clientèle is mainly local and over 60, although there is a sprinkling of younger people. The plump *patron* waiting on clients in his cloth cap is instantly recognisable, as there is a picture of him over the entrance next to the legend 'l'Ambiance d'Autrefois' ('the Atmosphere of Times Gone By'). This claim is borne out to a certain extent by the décor, the women's dresses, the 1960s music, the traditional menu and the prices. The food is certainly not haute cuisine but the *friture d'éperlans* (fried smelt, tiny fish very similar to whitebait) was garnished with garlic and parsley, and the *moules-frites* were freshly made. The waiter was so rushed off his feet by a large group celebrating a birthday that our *friture* and wine arrived without the bread and I despaired of ever getting any, after two fruitless visits to the kitchen and frantic reassurances by the waiter. Our newly-arrived

The patron of Chez Fifi

neighbour, a regular, was so touched by our plight that she got up and returned in triumph with a basket of bread for us, saying 'Ici, c'est à la bonne franquette'—'we don't stand on ceremony here'. The dancing starts at 3 pm and lasts until early evening so you could spend the entire afternoon at the guinguette, returning to Paris the way you came. You can order à la carte or just stop by for a drink. It is a relaxing place in which to sit in the sun at a table next to the river, watching the cormorants as well as the people. I once saw a water wagtail here, bobbing around at the water's edge.

Continue walking along the Marne towards the marina and the next bridge, where you can occasionally see huge barges going through the lock. Do not cross the bridge to the bland park on the other side but stay on the left to follow the narrow path beside the canal. The **Canal de Chelles** is quiet, shaded by trees, with only a few cyclists and strollers. On a hot day a few years ago I saw some boys jumping into the canal from the little iron bridge further on and happily splashing around in the water. The decaying bridge is now fenced off but the walk is still unpaved and feels like real countryside, with a wood and a stream on the left and buddleia growing by the water's edge. It is so overgrown by lush foliage in the summer that in parts of it you have to walk in single file. After about two kilometres you will pass a footbridge, a favourite spot for fishermen. Just after the next footbridge leave the canal by a little uphill path, as the towpath comes to an abrupt end soon afterwards.

Continue into a small road now closed to traffic, the rue du Chetivet. At the end of the road on the left is the 'Pointe de Gournay' stop for the **113 bus** which will take you to **Chelles-Gournay station**, four stops away. The time of the next bus is shown on the electronic indicator.

Lock at Canal de Chelles, Neuilly-sur-Marne

Optional 2.3 km walk to Chelles-Gournay station

However, if you want to prolong the walk you can take a less direct but almost traffic-free route to the station. Turn right from the rue du Chetivet, cross the main road at the pedestrian crossing, continue to the right, and take the first road on the left at the corner of the 'Speedy' garage, the quiet residential avenue Roger Salengro.

The road soon forks, so take the right-hand side which continues dead straight for almost a kilometre, with the railway line visible at the end. You will pass suburban houses, each with its little garden and a general air of modest prosperity. Just before the end, turn right into the avenue Ronsard, which becomes rue Pierre Dupont. Continue to the right of the little roundabout and take the boulevard Alsace-Lorraine, still quiet, but with bigger, older houses.

At the end of the boulevard turn left into the busy avenue du Maréchal Foch and continue for a little way. Go under the railway bridge, with its incongruous but imposing white neo-Doric columns, to find the **station** on the right.

There is a popular brasserie, **La Chelloise**, with a large terrace facing the station. I once ended up there on a sunny Sunday evening on 21 June, the Fête de la Musique, and was charmed by the sight of the local families, both French and immigrant, sitting together at tables outside. They had come to cheer on their teen-aged children who were performing with touching enthusiasm in an amateur concert on the station concourse.

Chelles-Gournay RER station opposite the brasserie is smart and modern and as soon as you step inside its glass doors you will be spiritually back in Paris. You can be physically back within 15 minutes.

Distance from Paris: 19 km (11½ miles)
Depart: Châtelet-Les Halles
Arrive: Neuilly-Plaisance
Journey time: 15 minutes
Length of visit: Half or full day
Alternative return from: Chelles-Gournay
Journey time: 14-28 minutes
Navigo Zone: 3 (Neuilly-Plaisance) and 4 (Chelles-Gournay)
Single ticket: 4.05€ (4.95€ from Chelles-Gournay)
Distance from Neuilly-Plaisance to Chez Fifi: 1 km (½ mile)
Distance from Chez Fifi to Pointe de Gournay bus stop: 2.8 km (1¾ miles)
Distance from bus stop to Chelles-Gournay station: 2.3 km (1½ miles)
Population: 34,763 (Neuilly-sur-Marne); 53,833 (Chelles)

Getting there

RER A trains to Marne-la-Vallée stopping at Neuilly-Plaisance run every 10 minutes.

Return from Chelles-Gournay: RER E stopping trains to Magenta (Gare du Nord) and Haussmann Saint-Lazare every 15 mins, 30 at weekends, taking 28 mins; fast SNCF trains to Gare de l'Est every 30 mins, taking 14 mins.

Bus 113 runs daily, every 5–20 mins depending on time of day.

Car: A4 to Joinville, then A86 to Le Perreux-sur-Marne and N34 to Neuilly-sur-Marne.

RATP map *plan de secteur, no. 11*. See p. 179.

When to go

Sunny weather is ideal to enjoy the play of sunlight on water. The atmosphere of the *guinguette* is at its most traditional on a Sunday in summer, when the transparent plastic 'walls' are rolled up to let in the sunshine, but you could go in winter as it is open all year round and cosily heated.

Useful information

For the addresses of other *guinguettes* near Paris, visit www.culture-guinguette.com.

Restaurants/cafés

Chez Fifi – Bar de la Marine, bar/restaurant, 2 rue Maurice Bertaux, 93330 Neuilly-sur-Marne, tel 01 43 08 20 31, mobile 06 81 52 91 04, www.guinguettechezfifi.fr/. Open daily all year round to 11 pm, dancing at weekends and public holidays 3–7 pm. Three-course *formule* including apéritif, wine and coffee, around 36€ or à la carte. *Friture d'éperlans* around 7€, traditional main dishes such as *moules-frites*, *choucroûte* or *tête de veau* 17€, 50cl *pichet* of quite drinkable rosé 9.80€. Admission to the dance floor without eating 10€, including a drink.

La Brasserie Chelloise, 71 avenue de la Résistance, 77500 Chelles, tel 01 60 20 50 71. Open daily to midnight, live music on Friday evenings.

6. Brunoy

A surprisingly rural walk along the River Yerres, past a neolithic menhir, a medieval mill and an 18th-century bridge to the country house of the Impressionist painter Caillebotte, set in a park by the river

The RER D station at Brunoy on the River Yerres looks like anywhere else when you get off the train, but not for long. Like many medieval villages on a tributary of the Seine close to Paris, the coming of the railway turned it into a suburb, with modern infrastructure disguising its ancient origins. But the closer you get to the river, the further back you journey in time and the more surprising and picturesque the walk becomes.

In the seventh century Brunoy was mentioned as a royal possession, prized for the good hunting to be had in the near-by Forêt de Sénart. Its famous château was demolished in the Revolution but it continued to attract wealthy Parisians who built several imposing country residences there in the 19th century, many still standing although nowadays put to public use. It is still essentially a residential town.

5 km walk along the River Yerres from Brunoy to Yerres

From Brunoy station take the place de la Gare exit, cross the road and continue straight ahead down the rue de la Gare which has a big brasserie/*tabac* on the corner. There are some decorative Art Nouveau touches on the houses at nos. 23 and 25.

At the end of the street turn right, past the modern Mediathèque and a small war memorial. You will see the spire of the medieval church above the skyline on your left. Turn left to face the grandiose Mairie (1898) set in a little square with an imposing plane tree in front of it and the **Tabac de la Mairie**

Gustave Caillebotte, 'Le parc, propriété Caillebotte', 1875

beside it in the Grande Rue on your right. This is a good place to stop for a drink, savouring the relaxed, almost provincial feel of the scene in front of you. In the Middle Ages this part of Brunoy with its 12th-century church, built on the site of an earlier one, was surrounded by a rampart along what is now the Grande Rue, and it is still the heart of the modern town.

With your back to the Tabac de la Mairie turn into the first street on the left, the little rue Pasteur, then take the first right, the tiny rue St-Nicolas. Turn left into a narrow un-named cobbled street, more like a passage, which will bring you to the back entrance of the **Eglise St Médard.** Turn right and go down steps into the square in front of you. The main entrance to the church is up the steps on your left. Built in the 12th, 13th and 16th centuries, embellished in the 18th century and restored in 2005, it is well worth a visit.

From its main entrance turn left down the rue Montmartel, follow it to the end and turn right downhill to the bridge ahead, the Pont Perronet. You will pass an old **mill** which is now a hotel, picturesquely framed by a weeping willow and a curved footbridge, on the site of an earlier mill which belonged to the château.

From the bridge turn left onto the Île de Brunoy, with a restaurant called **Le Pavillon de l'Île** on your right. It is a good place to have lunch as it is in a beautiful riverside setting. The

Gustave Caillebotte, 'L'Yerres, effet de pluie', 1875

French dishes were carefully cooked and reasonably priced, although it will have changed hands by the time you read this as its seven-year lease will expire soon. But as the local council owns the lease it seems likely that the restaurant will continue to offer good value to its main clientèle, the residents of Brunoy.

From the restaurant terrace there is an excellent view of the Neolithic menhir, **La Pierre Fritte**, on the opposite bank of the River Yerres facing a children's playground. The name derives from *la pierre fichée (figée) en terre*, literally 'stone stuck in the ground'. It dates from around 3000 BC but its function has remained a mystery and it is so small that you might easily overlook it. At 2.5 metres high, with another metre buried in the soil, it is the tallest stone visible of a group of three. There is a much smaller one next to it and a bigger one submerged in the river beneath it.

Next to the restaurant you will see a wooden barn, La Grange de l'Île, which dates from the 19th century and has been recently restored. You could continue for a little wander along the island, which has been turned into an attractive park with two picnic tables and paths along the Yerres on both sides, crossed by an impressive railway viaduct built in 1849.

Retrace your steps to the Pavillon de l'Île and cross the bridge to the other side of the river.

The Pont Perronet, built around 1784, is named after its engineer who also designed the Pont de la Concorde in Paris. It has a tasteful Greek border running along its parapet. Turn left and take the steps further along down from the bridge to follow the path, with the river on your right.

You will pass quite a few locals en route but the path feels rural rather than suburban, with towering trees, leaf-strewn paths, wild flowers, the sound of ducks and moorhens and possibly a glimpse of a heron. You will soon have another impressive view of the mill with the church at Brunoy behind it. The path ends at the picturesque **Pont de Soulins**, built in 1745 and painted by Caillebotte in 1874.

Cross the road and turn right onto the bridge. At the end

Pont de Soulins at Brunoy

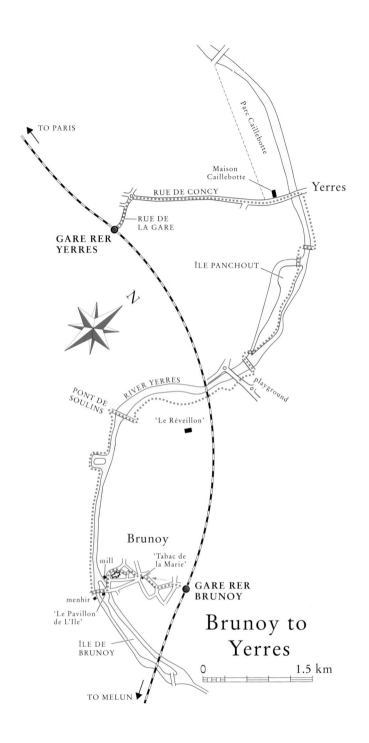

TO PARIS

Parc Caillebotte

Maison
Caillebotte

Yerres

RUE DE CONCY

RUE DE
LA GARE

GARE RER
YERRES

ÎLE PANCHOUT

N

playground

RIVER YERRES

PONT DE
SOULINS

'Le Réveillon'

Brunoy

mill   'Tabac de
              la Marie'

GARE RER
BRUNOY

menhir

'Le Pavillon
de L'Ile'

ÎLE DE
BRUNOY

Brunoy to
Yerres

0   1.5 km

TO MELUN

of the bridge follow the footpath on the left which leads to a gateway into the Parc de la Maison des Arts. The Maison is a villa, **Le Réveillon**, built in 1870 and now an arts centre, which you will eventually pass on your right. Continue to follow the riverside path which soon goes under another towering railway viaduct.

Take the first left across a footbridge and turn right. Cross another footbridge on the right and then turn left across a third footbridge and up an embankment onto a main road. Cross the road straight ahead of you, if you can (the pedestrian crossing is a little further to the right) to a small road directly opposite showing a height restriction of 1.90 metres for cars. This is the unmarked continuation of the river footpath, next to a children's playground in the Parc des Deux Rivières at Yerres. The ancient building visible to your right is a former abbey, now restored and turned into apartments.

Following the river, cross the next little footbridge over a dam and turn right to follow the Yerres onto the Île Panchout. There is a tempting little parallel path across a footbridge on the right but be warned that you will eventually be stopped by water and will have to turn back to rejoin the main path. There are extracts from poems along the main path which I personally found rather irritating, although well-intentioned. You may glimpse a fenced-off herd of Highland cattle, introduced here to crop the grass in an environmentally sustainable way.

Turn right across the next footbridge and continue to follow the river on your left. When you see a roadbridge ahead leave the path and take the steps on your right up to the bridge and a bus stop. Cross the road and turn left, over the river. The **Maison Caillebotte** is the white building straight ahead on the right.

The grounds, containing some remarkable trees, are now a public park. I have not visited the house but the grounds alone, which include the continuation of the riverside footpath, are worth the trip. The Caillebotte family bought the property in 1860 and spent their summers there until they sold it in 1879. It had been transformed by a previous owner in 1824 who turned the extensive grounds into a landscaped *jardin à l'anglaise*,

HALF AN HOUR FROM PARIS

complete with orangery, ice-house and other fashionable *fabriques*. The former 'chalet Suisse' now houses the restaurant and tea-room and the walled kitchen garden painted by Caillebotte in 1875 has been carefully restored and is run by volunteers. I can recommend the raspberries grown there, unfortunately not for sale but ripe for surreptitious plucking.

Like most of the owners of elegant villas in Brunoy and Yerres, Caillebotte *père* had made his fortune in Paris, in his case by supplying the French army with sheets and blankets. His second son, Gustave (1848–1894) became a talented painter of independent means, champion and patron of the Impressionists. The bucolic river and garden setting at Yerres inspired several of his early paintings. His outstanding collection of Impressionist paintings now forms the heart of the collection at the Musée d'Orsay.

To return to Paris turn right from the Maison Caillebotte onto the main road and continue on the right past La Grange au Bois, a 19th century villa in the then fashionable rustic style, now a music and dance conservatory, along the long rue de Concy. When you come to a roundabout, turn left into the rue de la Gare and continue uphill. Cross the road towards the bus stop and take steps up on the right to the **RER station** at Yerres.

Distance from Paris: 21 km (13 miles)
Depart: Châtelet-Les Halles
Arrive : Brunoy
Journey time : 32 minutes
Length of visit : Half or full day
Alternative return from: Yerres
Navigo Zone: 5
Single ticket: 5€
Distance from Brunoy to Yerres: 5 km (3 miles)
Population: 26,077

Getting there

RER D trains from Châtelet-Les Halles to Melun run every 15 minutes, stopping at Brunoy. Trains from Yerres run at the same frequency, taking 28 minutes to Châtelet-Les Halles.

Car: A4 from Porte de Bercy, then towards Mélun-Senart.

When to go

Sunny weather is preferable for this mainly outdoor visit. The Maison Caillebotte is open at weekends but the park is open daily.

Useful information

Propriété Caillebotte, 8 rue de Concy, 91330 Yerres, tel 01 80 37 20 61, www.maisoncaillebotte.fr The house is open at weekends 2–6.30 pm. Admission 8€, concessions 5€. Park open daily, admission free. Free 1½ hr guided visit of the *fabriques* and the kitchen garden at 3 pm on the first Sunday of the month, book by telephone or at the house.

Rowing boats and canoes for trips on the Yerres in the park can be hired from 3 pm at weekends and public holidays from June to October, from Tuesday to Sunday in August, from 7€ an hour.

Cafés and restaurants

Tabac de la Mairie, 4 place de la Mairie, 91800 Brunoy, tel 01 60 46 02 22. Closed on Wednesdays.

Le Pavillon de l'Île, 5 rue du Pont Perronet, Brunoy, tel 01 77 05 91 21. Open Wednesday-Sunday. Three-course menu 33€, two courses 27€ or à la carte. 25 cl *pichet* of wine 5.50€.

L'Orée du Parc, restaurant/tearoom in the Parc Caillebotte, tel 01 69 45 47 78. Open Wednesday-Sunday from 12.15 pm.

There are several restaurants and cafés in the attractive little town centre of Yerres clustered around its medieval church, over the bridge to the left of the Maison Caillebotte.

7. Igny

**A walk along the River Bièvre and tea in the garden
of the house-museum dedicated to Victor Hugo,
with the option of a short country walk to Jouy-en-Josas**

This is an easy walk along the quiet country stretch of an elusive little river, intimately bound up with the history of Paris. It still flows through Paris, but underground. You can visit the château des Roches, a country house frequented by Victor Hugo and Hector Berlioz near the River Bièvre, have tea there, and take the train back to Paris from Vauboyen station nearby. Or you can continue on a country walk of 2 km to find the river again at Jouy-en-Josas, where there is a mysterious Madonna in the 13th-century church, the house of the 18th-century entrepreneur Christophe-Philippe Oberkampf, who has a street and a métro station in Paris named after him, and a bar-restaurant with a garden where you can eat outside.

The hidden River Bièvre

The word 'Bièvre' comes from the Latin for beaver, although these animals, once very active in this river, had been hunted to extinction by the 13th century. Rarely more than three metres wide, the Bièvre is a tributary of the Seine, with its source at Guyancourt, 20 km west of Paris. For centuries it flowed for 33 km from Guyancourt through to the south of Paris, joining the Seine where the Gare d'Austerlitz now stands, not far from Notre Dame. The Roman name for Paris, Lutetia, comes from a Gallic word meaning 'marsh', probably from the ancient marsh near the Jardin des Plantes formed by the Bièvre, always prone to flooding.

By the 19th century the pollution of the Bièvre in Paris by

The River Bièvre at Igny

dyers and tanners had turned it into a serious health hazard. It was progressively covered over and its waters became part of the Paris sewage system. It now flows underground from Antony, 20 km south of Paris, through the 5th and 13th *arrondissements* and under the rue de la Bièvre before joining the Seine. There was actually a recent project to return the Bièvre to its original open riverbed through Paris, until the ruinous cost caused it to be abandoned. But the alarming effects of climate change and the role played by open water in cooling densely-populated urban areas has reversed that decision. The city of Paris is planning to uncover two stretches of the Bièvre in the 13th arrondissement by 2026, with more stretches of the river to follow.

Jouy-en-Josas partly owes its present prosperity to the Bièvre, as it was the purity of its waters at this spot as well as its proximity to Versailles and Paris that led Oberkampf, a 22-year-old German from a family of artisanal dyers, to set up his textile dyeing workshop in a modest house by the river at Jouy in 1760. The fabric was rinsed several times in the Bièvre and spread out to dry in the surrounding meadows. The town soon became famous for the production of colour-fast printed cotton in a variety of fashionable designs, 'Les Toiles de Jouy'. By 1805 the dyeing works had been mechanised, employing over a thousand workers, more than half the population of Jouy, and had become one of the largest manufactories in France, eventually spreading over 14 hectares. But the devastation caused by the Napoleonic wars and Oberkampf's death in 1815 were followed by the rise of competition from cheaper centres of production. Demand steadily declined and La Manufacture des Toiles de Jouy ceased production in 1843. The vast site was sold off and only the rising popularity of Jouy as a weekend destination saved the town from economic collapse.

Its picturesque setting started to attract Parisians in the 19th century. Victor Hugo rented a room there in 1834 for his mistress Juliette Drouet while he stayed with his family at the château des Roches nearby, and Léon Blum retired to Jouy, where he died in 1950. Today it is still picturesque, although rather too quiet on Sundays. It is the site of the prestigious HEC (Hautes Etudes Commerciales) school of management and of several important research and training establishments such as INRA (Institut National de la Recherche Agronomique) and Thales, the French multinational defence contractor.

4 km walk from Igny station via the Maison littéraire de Victor Hugo to Vauboyen station

Take the underpass from the platform, 'sortie avenue Jean Jaurès'. Do a U-turn from the underpass to turn left towards the wood and then right into a small downhill path with a car barrier and yellow PR sign (see pp. 177-178). It soon brings you to the little River Bièvre. Turn left to follow the river until you come to a small road and cross it to continue along the riverside footpath. This is the prettiest part of the walk. You will hear birdsong, perhaps see a few ducks and pass local walkers out for a stroll. Bear left to continue past quite a large pond with ducks and herons, a good place for a picnic.

Continue to another gate at a small road and follow the red and white GR sign left into the Route de Verrières. Follow the

Maison littéraire de Victor Hugo

road round to the right and under the road bridge ahead. At the pedestrian crossing you will see a little path on your right with a GR/PR right turn sign. Follow the path, taking the first left turn, past modern apartment blocks on your left, then across a wooden footbridge with a little waterfall opposite. Celandines grow here in spring and cowslips a little further on at the weir. You will pass a sign saying 'Gare' on your left, pointing to a footpath which leads to the **station at Bièvres**. Continue along the river until you come to steps up to a road. The river goes through the little tunnel on your right and cannot be followed after this point.

Turn left and cross the road at the pedestrian crossing into the rue des Prés on the right. There is a little shop at this corner, open daily except between 1.30 and 3.30 pm, where you can buy cold beer and picnic supplies. Follow the rue des Prés to the very end, across a small road and continue straight on along the chemin des Prés de Vauboyen, a pretty little path where I have seen snowdrops and periwinkles growing in spring. Ignore the PR right turn sign for 'Maison Victor Hugo' and continue straight on until you come to a little weir and a sign explaining the literary and artistic associations of the Bièvre at this rural spot—Satie, Berlioz, Ingres, Corot, Rabelais, Rousseau and Chateaubriand all drew inspiration from it, as well as Victor Hugo. Cross the footbridge over the Bièvre at the weir and follow the narrow path ahead straight on uphill to the end, skirting a wall on your right and across another footbridge, until you come out onto a main road.

The entrance to the elegant little château des Roches, now known as the **Maison littéraire de Victor Hugo**, is immediately on your left. Built in the 18th century, in 1804 it was acquired by Louis-François Bertin, founder and editor of the royalist *Journal des débats*. Between 1815 and his death in 1841 he turned it into a literary salon where Hugo, Berlioz, Gounod, Ingres, Liszt, and Chateaubriand, who lived nearby, were frequent guests. It is now owned by a Japanese Buddhist charity which has opened it to the public.

The guided visit lasts 45 minutes, in French, but the groups are never very large. As well as the corrected proofs of *Les Misérables,* the display includes a letter from Berlioz and a list of the household expenses of Juliette Drouet, Hugo's mistress. They are addressed to 'Toto' from 'Juju'. In the Salon Rouge are displayed Hugo's last words, three days before he died in 1885 at the age of 83: 'Aimer, c'est agir' (To love is to act). But for me an equally rewarding aspect of the visit is the quiet 10-hectare landscaped **park** which overlooks the river and is crossed by a little stream, below the **tea-room** which has tables outside. There is a romantic view of the valley of the Bièvre from the stone balustrade of the tea-room terrace, and you can play the piano inside and think of the musicians who came here. The cakes are good, too.

Return to the footpath at the right of the entrance and follow it downhill back to the weir. Turn right along the riverside path, which is signed 'Sentier Maurice et Alain-Victor Marchand, GR11 Sentier de la Bièvre', parallel to the railway line on the left. Continue for about ten minutes, when you will come to a small road and the entrance to the **station at Vauboyen**.

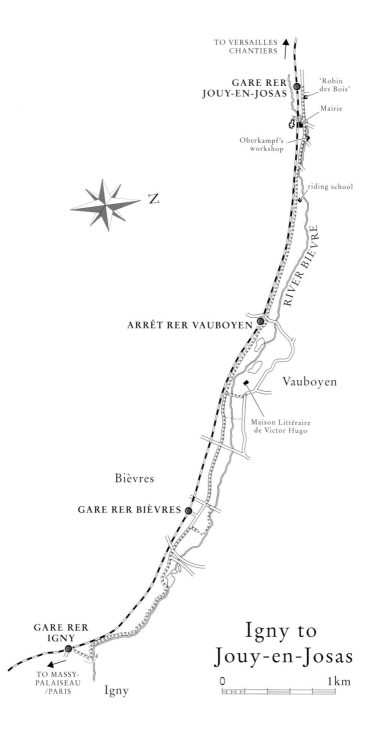

TO VERSAILLES
CHANTIERS

**GARE RER
JOUY-EN-JOSAS**

'Robin
des Bois'

Mairie

Oberkampf's
workshop

riding school

RIVER BIÈVRE

ARRÊT RER VAUBOYEN

Vauboyen

Maison Littéraire
de Victor Hugo

Bièvres

GARE RER BIÈVRES

Z

**GARE RER
IGNY**

TO MASSY-
PALAISEAU
/PARIS

Igny

Igny to
Jouy-en-Josas

0   1km

Optional 2.3 km walk from Vauboyen to Jouy-en-Josas

You can prolong the short peaceful walk to Jouy-en-Josas, where the elusive Bièvre reappears. Turn right, cross the road and take the first left into the chemin de Vauboyen, a continuation of the footpath parallel to the railway line.

Keep close to the line, ignoring a tempting wider path to your right, which leads to the uphill GR road route to Jouy-en-Josas. The narrow footpath is prettier, easier and traffic-free as well as shorter, although it can be muddy in winter. You are unlikely to meet a soul and the only sound is an occasional train. Eventually you will pass a pedestrian crossing over the railway line, closed by a gate. The gate has a faded old SNCF sign with a black and white illustration which must date from the 1940s or 50s, showing a careless father who has led his family into danger, in the process of reeling backwards and losing his hat as a train rushes towards him. His wife, holding her son's hand and carrying a baby, is wearing an apron and high heels. 'Do not cross without looking both ways', it warns: 'un train peut en cacher un autre' ('one train can hide another').

After passing a riding school on your right you will come to a concrete footbridge over the Bièvre. The path now becomes a road which goes past one of the INRA buildings on the left, which looks like an old-fashioned little railway station. Follow the road, which crosses the Bièvre, and keep to the right as the road joins the main road into Jouy, the avenue Jean Jaurès. Take the first street on the right across the river, the short rue du Thabot, which leads into the rue de la Manufacture des Toiles de Jouy.

Turn left and continue to the very end of the street, where you will see a little house labelled 'Ecole de Musique' facing the Bièvre. The entrance has the date 1760 carved over the door, as it was **Oberkampf's workshop** and modest first home at Jouy. He and his family are buried beneath the obelisks in the garden. Continue past the garden to rejoin the main road, avenue Jean Jaurès, and turn right.

Continue until you see the imposing **Mairie** opposite and cross the road. Built for Oberkampf in 1766, it was here that he

La Diège, Jouy-en-Josas

entertained guests such as Marie-Antoinette and then Napoleon after becoming Jouy's first citizen-Mayor in 1790. He died here in 1815. His bust stands in the courtyard at the back of the Mairie, just before the level crossing.

Continue over the level crossing into the rue Oberkampf and just before the end of the street turn left to find the **Eglise St Martin**, hidden in a quiet square. The oldest part of the church is 13th-century, with modifications dating from the Renaissance. The softly lit 12th-century statue of the Madonna known as **'La Diège'** is to the right, glowing in the dim church. 'Diège' is a contraction of Dei Genitrix, 'Mother of God'. She is now enclosed in a glass case, but at least this means that the church is always open, and the statue has preserved its air of mystery. I was not surprised to discover that it was the object of a pilgrimage during the Middle Ages. It is unique in that it shows Christ as a child standing in front of his mother holding the globe, rather than as a baby held on her lap. That his kingdom is not of this world is symbolised by his feet being held aloft by two angels. La Diège originally held a rose, now missing, in her hand, a symbol of intercession and maternal love. The statue was walled up in a farmhouse for safe-keeping during the Revolution, where it was subsequently forgotten. It was rediscovered by chance in 1850 and installed in this church.

Return to the level crossing, go over it back into the avenue Jaurès and turn left. The entrance to the **station at Jouy-en-Josas** is a little further on, just past the **Robin des Bois** ('Robin Hood') bar-restaurant opposite. The best thing about the Robin des Bois, apart from the fact that it is open on Sunday, is the garden, where you can order a simple plate of home-made *frites* washed down with ice-cold beer or just a coffee.

Distance from Paris: 17 km (10½ miles)
Depart: Châtelet-Les Halles
Arrive: Igny
Journey time: 37 minutes
Length of visit: Half or full day
Return from: Bièvres, Vauboyen or Jouy-en-Josas
Navigo Zone: 4
Single ticket: 4.05€ (4.95€ from Bièvres, Vauboyen or Jouy-en-Josas)
Distance from Igny to Bièvres: 2 km (1.2 miles)
Distance from Bièvres to Vauboyen: 2 km (1.2 miles)
Distance from Vauboyen to Jouy-en-Josas: 2¼ km (1.3 miles)
Population: 10,228 (Igny); 8,291 (Jouy-en-Josas)

Getting there

RER B trains run approximately every 15 minutes from Châtelet-Les Halles to St-Rémy-lès-Chevreuse, stopping at Massy-Palaiseau around 26 minutes later.

At Massy-Palaiseau change to an RER C train to Versailles-Chantiers to travel one stop to Igny, with around seven minutes to make the connection.

NB: Check the SNCF website for the connecting train before setting off, as RER C trains from Massy-Palaiseau to Versailles-Chantiers are hourly on Sunday mornings, half-hourly at other times. The station at Massy-Palaiseau is huge, as it serves RER lines B and C and is next door to the TGV Atlantique station, so don't dawdle while making the change. If you miss the train on a Sunday morning and have to wait for an hour, there is a baker in the market at the bus station exit on the right where you can buy coffee to take away.

On the return trip RER C trains from Bièvres, Vauboyen and Jouy-en-Josas run every half hour to Massy-Palaiseau, from where there are more frequent RER B trains to Paris. Check the train indicator at Massy-Palaiseau to see if all the stations are lit up, meaning the train stops at each one of them, and if necessary choose a later train which skips some stations as it will probably get into Paris sooner. The fastest journey time from Jouy-en-Josas to Châtelet-Les Halles is 48 minutes.

Car: N118 from Pont de Sèvres, exit Bièvres for the Maison Littéraire de Victor Hugo.

When to go

Mild weather is preferable for this mainly outdoor visit, although you could cut the walking by taking the train to Vauboyen and just visiting the Maison Littéraire de Victor Hugo nearby, which is open for most of the year.

If you plan to walk there from Igny take a train which arrives no earlier than 1 pm, as the château is only open from 2.30 pm at weekends, and the walk takes not much more than an hour. You could of course turn your walk into a leisurely stroll and picnic by the river, or in the château park after 2.30 pm.

If it is Sunday, the only source of food or drink on this walk, apart from the little shop at Bièvres and the tea-room at the Maison Hugo, is the Robin des Bois in Jouy-en-Josas where the kitchen closes at 2.30 pm and re-opens at 6 pm, or La Medina, a Moroccan restaurant in the rue Oberkampf near the church, with similar hours. The church is always open.

Useful information

Maison littéraire de Victor Hugo, Château des Roches, 45 rue de Vauboyen, 91570 Bièvres, tel 01 69 41 82 84, http://www.maisonlitterairedevictorhugo.net/. Open at weekends between March and November 2.30–6.30 pm or at other times for groups of at least 10 by arrangement. Admission, including the park, 6€, 5€ for children under 12, students, people over 60 and groups. Admission to the park only, 3€.

Restaurants and cafés

Robin des Bois bar/restaurant, 38 avenue Jean Jaurès, 78350 Jouy-en-Josas, tel 01 39 56 40 34, https://le-robin.fr. Open daily for lunch and dinner, closed between 3 and 6 pm. Specialises in *pierrades* at around 20€, thin strips of raw beef which you cook yourself on a heated griddle at the table. 25 cl *pichet* of acceptable Côtes du Rhône, 5€.

Salon de thé, Maison Littéraire de Victor Hugo. Open at the same times as the château, it has a terrace overlooking the valley of the Bièvre and a piano inside which guests can play. The tiny cakes are good value and there is a pleasing ceremoniousness about the service.

8. Château de Vincennes

A 14th-century royal fortress, lunch in a 1950s brasserie and an optional woodland walk through the Bois de Vincennes to the abandoned colonial pavilions of the Jardin Tropical

Situated just outside Paris in the Bois de Vincennes, the Château de Vincennes has preserved its 14th-century appearance, a walled fortress surrounded by parkland. Rather like the Tower of London, it has been in turn royal residence and stronghold, seat of government, prison and arsenal and is now a state-run museum. Perhaps because it is so close to Paris it is often overlooked, by Parisians and foreign visitors alike. Their loss, your gain.

Lunch in the long established two-star hotel-brasserie opposite the métro, surrounded by local families, feels like eating in a traditional Paris brasserie, c. 1950. Its splendid art deco circular skylight, cosy seating, traditional menus, reasonable prices and unpretentious ambiance add to the pleasure of discovering the château. You could round off the visit by taking a woodland path through the Bois de Vincennes, past a boating lake to visit the abandoned pavilions of the 1907 'Exposition Coloniale', hidden in the Jardin Tropical on the edge of the Bois and a rather well-kept secret, returning to Paris from the nearby RER station of Nogent-sur-Marne.

The Château de Vincennes

The development of a 12th-century hunting lodge in the Bois of Vincennes into an important fortified royal residence in the 14th century was probably the result of two factors: the absorption of the nearby county of Champagne into the kingdom of France in 1284, increasing the importance of Paris; and its convenient location close to the River Seine and the old Roman road from

The bridge to the donjon, Château de Vincennes

Paris to Sens. This allowed the medieval monarchs easy access to other parts of their kingdom and enabled the necessary supplies to reach the château.

It was and still is dominated by the 50-metre high donjon (castle keep), the castle within a castle which is the tallest building of its type still standing in Europe and the highlight of the visit. The decision to fortify Vincennes was a result of the Hundred Years' War with the English, during which Jean II ('Le Bon', 1350-1364) was taken prisoner and had to be ransomed at vast expense. The need to protect the king and the access to Paris, as well as explosive social unrest at home, in the shape of the bourgeois revolt in Paris led by Etienne Marcel and 'la Jacquerie', the peasants' revolt north of Paris, both in 1358, explain the speed and thoroughness with which the work was carried out. The donjon was started in 1361 and completed by 1371 under Charles V ('Le Sage', 1364-1380) and the deep moat and three-metre thick walls incorporating nine towers 40 metres high surrounding the whole complex were finished by 1380.

The donjon was used by Charles V to run his medieval kingdom from a permanent impregnable base: his private apartments, including a treasure room where sacks of gold were kept, were linked by a staircase to the council chamber one floor below, which also doubled as a spare bedroom. This monarch has been credited with creating a new form of government in which the king was surrounded by a few trusted advisors and secretaries, effectively a cabinet. His arrangement of the vertical space dictated by the shape of the square defensive tower is what visitors still see today, offering a memorable glimpse into the heart of a late medieval government. Some have seen in it the beginnings of the centralised modern French state.

Following the Battle of Agincourt in 1415, the victorious English king Henry V became the heir-apparent to the French throne, and in 1420 made the Château de Vincennes his main residence, from where he could control Paris and the Île de France. He even carried out some repairs there, before dying unexpectedly at the age of 35 in the donjon in 1422. The kings of France continued to visit Vincennes sporadically but after the 15th century the donjon was no longer used as a seat of government. The last major architectural re-modelling of the site by Le Vau and Le Nôtre was for the marriage of Louis XIV in 1660. After 1682 when the court moved to Versailles, Vincennes more or less ceased to be a royal residence. It had already been used to house a few high-ranking prisoners in conditions of some comfort, such as Henri de Navarre (the future Henri IV), and this continued until the end of the Ancien Régime; inmates included the Cardinal de Retz, Nicolas Fouquet, Voltaire, the Marquis de Sade, Mirabeau and Diderot. Some of the drawings and graffitti left by the prisoners can still be seen on the walls.

After the Revolution the château became a barracks, which Napoleon decided to strengthen by having seven of the remaining eight towers lopped to form platforms for artillery. It continued to be used as an arsenal and prison during the 19th century, when the Sainte-Chapelle was restored by Viollet-le-Duc. Restoration started on the donjon in the 1930s. The Sainte-Chapelle and the donjon were the only buildings to survive the blowing up of the château by the Germans during the retreat from Normandy in August 1944. It seems that the German sapper in charge of the operation could not bring himself to carry out his orders.

Today the château houses the archives of the French armed forces and is jointly run by the Ministries of Defence and of Culture. De Gaulle considered using it as the presidential residence, although nothing came of the plan. But its importance in the history of France is reflected in the extensive state-funded restoration of the donjon as a museum between 1995 and 2007 despite its few, mainly French, visitors.

The Jardin Tropical

The 4½ hectare 'Jardin Tropical' is hidden at the eastern edge of the Bois de Vincennes, 3 km from the château. It was created in 1899 for the scientific cultivation and study of rubber, coffee, cocoa, banana and vanilla plants, which were then sent to the French colonies in Africa and Asia to improve the crops being grown there. In 1907 Tuareg, Indo-Chinese, Madagascan, Congolese, Sudanese and New Caledonian 'colonial villages' were recreated in the Jardin Tropical for the 'Exposition Coloniale' which attracted two million visitors between May

Entrance to the Jardin Tropical, Bois de Vincennes

Memorial to soldiers from Madagascar, 1918, Jardin Tropical

and October. The decaying *pavillons* dotting the park are the remains of these artificial villages.

During the First World War soldiers from the colonies were treated in a hospital in the Jardin Tropical, and after the war memorials to those who died fighting for France were erected there. The site was then used by various horticultural research centres until 1995 but tropical plants were no longer grown there. The abandoned buildings continued to decay and some were vandalised.

In 2003 the site was acquired by the City of Paris and has been open to the public since 2006, although not many people seem to know about it. It is listed as of historical significance but until quite recently a general air of neglect pervaded the whole place and gave it a perfectly unique atmosphere. Since the first edition of this book some attempt has been made to make more of the site, with more explanatory notices (in French) and a general tidying-up of the undergrowth. But it has retained its slightly melancholy and mysterious atmosphere.

Suggested visit to the château

Leave the métro by the 'Château de Vincennes' exit. You will be hit in the eye by the château as soon as you emerge. Follow the signs to the main entrance and the ticket office.

The donjon

Climb the stairs to the Terrasse and the chemin de Ronde from which there is a good **view** of the whole walled site before crossing the footbridge to the donjon itself. There are clear explanatory notices throughout, in French, English and Spanish and a reproduction of the illustration for December from the famous book of hours, *Les Très Riches Heures du Duc de Berry*, c. 1440,

The Château de Vincennes, seen in the miniature representing December, from Les Très Riches Heures du Duc de Berry, c. 1440

which shows the Duke's birthplace, the Château de Vincennes with its nine towers, in the background. There are graffitti and designs carved by prisoners on the walls here, dating from the 17th century.

Leading off from Charles V's huge bedroom on the second floor to the right of the fireplace is a revealing series of smaller, more private rooms: his chapel and oratory, treasure room and isolated study with a view over Paris, and a discreet latrine next to it. Don't miss the small room to the left of the fireplace, the **king's wardrobe**, decorated with sculpted angel-musicians playing the lute, the bagpipes and other instruments. If you press the button below each one you will hear medieval music played on the selected instrument, a pleasing touch.

The third floor is open for a guided visit at 11 am on Sundays, where a notice in French warns you that there are 250 steps. I haven't tried this. Descending to the ground floor you will see a huge well and informative notices about the famous prisoners who were incarcerated here. The Marquis de Sade's cell is to the left, with a slide projection onto the wall of the letters he wrote to his wife from prison, with an English translation. Cross the courtyard for an audio-visual presentation of the history of the château (in French) and a model which gives you a useful impression of the whole complex as it was originally designed.

La Sainte-Chapelle

A turning point in the rise in importance of Vincennes was the decision of Louis IX (St Louis, 1226–1270) to deposit several important holy relics of Christ's Passion there. These were eventually housed in the Sainte-Chapelle opposite the donjon, modelled on the one in Paris. It was begun in 1379 but only completed in 1552. This comparatively late date and the fact that it consists of only one floor may explain why it doesn't quite have the impressive atmosphere of the Paris Sainte-Chapelle. It does have two helpful models of the appearance of the site in the 14th and 17th centuries.

The ceiling of the Terminus Château brasserie

Return to the main entrance, cross the main road and turn right for the Terminus Château hotel/brasserie, opposite métro exit 4 (Fort Neuf) and flanked by other, more expensive restaurants. You will probably be the only non-French visitors, although they do have a menu in English. Do not be put off by this, nor by the pictures of dishes displayed at the entrance. The service is brisk and attentive, but the decor and the atmosphere are decidedly old-fashioned, in spite of the TV screens, with multi-generational families enjoying leisurely traditional dishes such as *gigot d'agneau* (roast leg of lamb) and *petit salé aux lentilles* (salted knuckle of pork with lentils) at very reasonable prices. It is the kind of traditional Paris brasserie that is fast disappearing from Paris.

From here you can return to Paris in minutes via **métro line 1**, or rather more slowly by **bus 46** or **56**, both of which go to Gare de l'Est and Gare du Nord. The bus station is opposite, at métro exit 4.

Optional 3 km walk via the Jardin Tropical to Nogent-sur-Marne station

If you want to continue exploring, I highly recommend the woodland walk through the Bois de Vincennes to the Jardin Tropical. Cross the main road from the Terminus Château brasserie back towards the château and continue straight on, past the château on your right, until you come to a junction, with the Parc Floral facing you. Turn left into a pretty woodland path, the avenue des Minimes, signed 'Nogent 2,700m'. The path eventually curves right and continues over a main road, the avenue du Tremblay. Keep going until you see two red and white brick buildings ahead, which means you have arrived at the **Lac des Minimes**, just behind them.

Take the lakeside footpath and follow the lake round to the right, a very pretty woodland walk, past little beaches, ducks and swans, and rowing boats on sunny weekends. When you come to a clearing with a huge tree in the middle surrounded by a fence, go towards the tree and turn left to continue along the bigger avenue, the Route Circulaire, ignoring the Route de la Cascade ahead to your right.

At the next intersection with a paved road a little further on, turn right onto the Route de la Ménagerie, with a little stream on your right. Continue along this car-free road, ignoring the eventual sign on your right for the Jardin Tropical (it leads to a side entrance which is closed on weekdays, and is less impressive than the main entrance). Keep going until you see a little footbridge over the stream on your right, with no sign. Cross it, continue along the path to the end and turn right into the main entrance of the **Jardin Tropical**, through which you can see a faded red Chinese archway decorated with dragons and phoenixes.

This is your first hint of the exotic pavilions, bridges and decaying statues which are dotted around this small park within a park and are at their most mysterious on weekdays when there are scarcely any visitors. To the right of the archway you are in Asia, to the left in Africa. Whichever continent you choose, it is easy to circle round the park, crossing the little stream which runs through it to arrive back at your starting point.

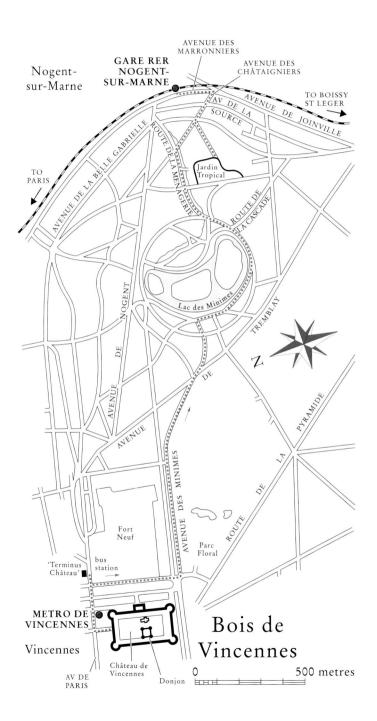

Nogent-sur-Marne

AVENUE DES MARRONNIERS

AVENUE DES CHÂTAIGNIERS

GARE RER NOGENT-SUR-MARNE

AV DE LA SOURCE

AVENUE DE JOINVILLE

TO BOISSY ST LEGER

TO PARIS

AVENUE DE LA BELLE GABRIELLE

ROUTE DE LA MÉNAGERIE

Jardin Tropical

ROUTE DE LA CASCADE

AVENUE DE NOGENT

Lac des Minimes

TREMBLAY

N

AVENUE DE

AVENUE DES MINIMES

ROUTE DE LA PYRAMIDE

Fort Neuf

'Terminus Château'

bus station

Parc Floral

ROUTE DE LA

METRO DE VINCENNES

Vincennes

AV DE PARIS

Château de Vincennes

Donjon

Bois de Vincennes

0   500 metres

To reach the **RER station at Nogent-sur-Marne**, cross the road opposite the main entrance and go straight on down the avenue des Châtaigniers, signed 'RER A', to the end. Turn left into the avenue des Marronniers and you will see the station at the end, on the right.

Distance from Paris: 6½ km (4 miles)
Depart: Châtelet, métro Line 1
Arrive: Château de Vincennes (terminus)
Journey time: 17 minutes
Length of visit: Half or full day
Alternative return from: Nogent-sur-Marne RER A
Navigo Zone: 2 (Zone 3 for Nogent-sur-Marne)
Single ticket: 2.10€ (3.10€ from Nogent-sur-Marne)
Distance from Château de Vincennes to Nogent-sur-Marne station: 3 km (1.8 miles)
Population of Vincennes: 49,695

Getting there

Métro Line 1 from central Paris terminates at the château de Vincennes stop opposite the château and is the quickest way to get there. RER A Vincennes station is a little further from the château.

Buses 46 and **56** also terminate there from central Paris.

Return from Nogent-sur-Marne: RER A trains run roughly every 15 minutes, taking 14 minutes to Châtelet-Les Halles.

Car: D120 Porte de Vincennes and avenue de Paris.

RATP maps *plans de secteur, nos. 10 and 12*. See p. 179.

When to Go

You could go at any time of the year or the week, as the château, the Terminus Château brasserie and the Jardin Tropical are open daily, but the Bois de Vincennes gets quite crowded on sunny weekends. Arguably, it is at its most beautiful in autumn. A good time to visit the donjon is at lunch time when there are even fewer people and the Sainte-Chapelle is closed. You could visit the Sainte-Chapelle before 1 pm or between 2 and 5.30 pm.

Useful information

Office de Tourisme de Vincennes, opposite the château at 28 avenue de Paris, 94300 Vincennes, tel 01 48 08 13 00, http://www.vincennes-tourisme. fr. Closed on Mondays, Sundays, holidays and on Thursday mornings. Open 9.30 am–12.30 pm and 1.30–5.30 pm, 6.30 pm in summer. Open on Thursday mornings in July and August.

Château de Vincennes, 1 avenue de Paris, Vincennes, tel 01 48 08 31 20, http://www.chateau-de-vincennes.fr/en. Open daily except on 1 Jan, 1 May and 25 Dec: 10 am–5 pm, 6 pm in summer. The

Sainte-Chapelle is open 10.30 am–1 pm and 2–4.30 pm, 5.30 pm in summer. Admission 9.50€, free to under 18s, to EU residents under 26 and to everyone on the first Sunday of the month between November and March.

NB: You can download a brochure with some useful historical information in English from the website. Click on 'We wish you a very good visit', then on 'Guide booklet' and select English.

Jardin Tropical de Bois de Vincennes, 45 bis avenue de la Belle Gabrielle, 75012 Paris. www. paris.fr/equipements/jardin-d-agronomie-tropicale-rene-dumont-1813. Open daily 9.30 am to 8 pm in summer, closes between 5 and 7 pm in winter. Admission free.

Cafés and restaurants

You can buy picnic supplies in the side streets of Vincennes near the market opposite the château, an area which is rapidly gentrifying.

Le Terminus Château hotel/brasserie/café, 9 avenue de Nogent, Vincennes, tel 01 48 08 40 58, www.facebook.com/leterminus chateau. Open daily until 11 pm, non-stop service. *Plats du jour* 13€, 3-course menu 18.50€, 25 cl *pichet* of drinkable *vin de pays* 5€.

9. Parc Saint-Cloud

A short walk of discovery through a historic but little-known park overlooking the Seine at Sèvres near Paris, past two very different museums and the old town of Saint-Cloud

On a hill overlooking a bend of the Seine to the west of Paris, the vast Parc Saint-Cloud, which once surrounded a royal château, is nowadays mainly frequented by locals. But this short bucolic walk with its sweeping views of the river and the city offers Parisians and visitors a real sense of *dépaysement* ('change of scene'), at the end of a métro line.

En route you are transported from the classical 17th century French formality of the Grande Cascade waterfall with its panoramic views of Paris to the romantic hilltop Jardin de Trocadéro designed *à l'anglaise* in the early 19th century as a private retreat for the children of the royal family. At the start and end of the walk you will pass two interesting and very different museums, with the chance to see some beautiful Sèvres porcelain. The walk continues through the quiet little streets of the old hillside town of Saint-Cloud with its church containing the relics of the sixth-century saint who gave the town and the park his name. From there you descend by a series of steps to a range of transport options, including the 72 bus which follows the right bank of the Seine in Paris from the Pont Mirabeau to the Île St Louis, giving you an armchair view of some of the city's most iconic sights.

3½ km walk from Pont de Sèvres to Saint-Cloud

Take métro line 9 to its terminus at Pont de Sèvres and leave by exit 2, quai Alphonse Le Gallo. Turn left, cross the road and turn right onto the main road leading to the Pont de Sèvres, staying on the right-hand side across the bridge.

Etienne Allegrain, 'View of château and park at St-Cloud', 1675

You will see an egg-shaped glass-covered dome to your left on the Île Séguin, a useful landmark. It is the auditorium of La Seine Musicale, a music and performing arts centre which opened in 2017. The building ahead on the other side of the river, surmounted by a clock and looking rather like a 19th century railway station, is the **Musée de Sèvres** on the edge of the Parc Saint-Cloud.

Ignore the steps down from the bridge marked 'Musée de Sèvres'. Instead, continue a little way and at the bus stop turn right to follow the pedestrian signs for 'Musée Céramique' downhill. This walkway takes you over the busy main road to the museum entrance.

The museum's huge national collection has been organised to tell the story of the art of pottery, with beautiful examples drawn from every period and every country, but with pride of place given to the porcelain which has been produced at the state-owned Manufacture de Sèvres since 1759. It is never crowded and well worth a visit, even a brief one, to see some masterpieces of the potter's art displayed in their historical context.

Turn left from the entrance and continue to a gate which

Sèvres porcelain, 18th century, Musée de Sèvres

leads into the Parc Saint-Cloud, of which the 4 hectares occupied by the museum were once a part. I have never forgotten the
sense of exhilaration I felt when I first visited this museum on an
impulsive escape from Paris and discovered the entrance to the
unsuspected 490-hectare park next door. Just to the left of the
gate there is a discreet WC, unmarked but identifiable by a water
tap outside. Turn left here and then take the first right to follow
a tree-lined path, parallel to the riverside footpath but less close
to the busy road.

In the 16th century a château stood halfway up this hill
with gardens sloping down to the Seine. The setting was so attractive that in 1658 Louis XIV bought the château and its 12
hectares of parkland for his younger brother, the 18-year-old
Philippe d'Orléans. By the time 'Monsieur' died in 1701 the
original château had been absorbed into the fabric of a much
grander building and the park, re-designed by Le Nôtre, had
expanded to an enormous 590 hectares. The finishing touches
to the Grande Cascade staircase waterfall were added by Jules
Hardouin-Mansart in 1690. The hillside setting with its sweeping views of the Seine is visually more dramatic than Versailles,

but without the crowds. Since 1870 it has also been without the château, although since 2012 an association has been lobbying for its reconstruction.

The château de Saint-Cloud was a favourite country retreat with its successive royal and imperial owners, including Marie Antoinette, Napoleon I and Napoleon III. It was the setting for Napoleon's coup d'état in 1799 and for that of his nephew in 1852. It was from Saint-Cloud that Napoleon III made his ill-fated declaration of war on Prussia in 1870. Two months later the château had become the headquarters of the Prussian army besieging Paris and was bombarded by the French from the nearby fort of Mont-Valérien. One of their shells fell into the Emperor's apartments and started a fire which burned for two days. It seems that the Prussians were not displeased by this turn of events and did nothing to put it out. Twenty years later the burnt-out ruins, a sad reminder of defeat, were finally dismantled by the French state, which owns the park.

Walk straight on, always taking the left when the path forks, past a pompous group of statues ('France crowning Art and Industry', 1900) until you come to the 90-metre long **Grande Cascade**, the most visually dramatic ensemble in the

The Grande Cascade

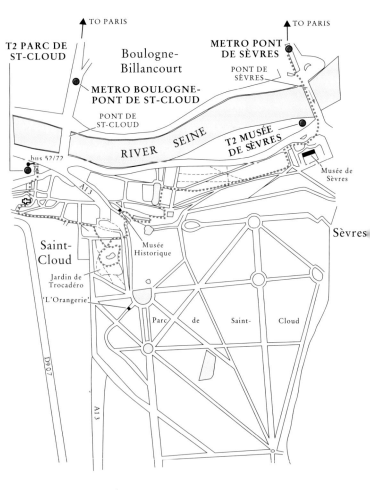

TO PARIS

**T2 PARC DE
ST-CLOUD**

Boulogne-
Billancourt

**METRO PONT
DE SÈVRES**

TO PARIS

PONT DE
SÈVRES

**METRO BOULOGNE-
PONT DE ST-CLOUD**

PONT DE
ST-CLOUD

RIVER   SEINE

**T2 MUSÉE
DE SÈVRES**

bus 52/72

A13

Musée de
Sèvres

Sèvres

Saint-
Cloud

Musée
Historique

Jardin de
Trocadéro

'L'Orangerie'

Parc   de   Saint-   Cloud

D907

A13

Parc de
Saint-Cloud

0   500 metres

N

park. Take the left-hand path to the top and turn left, then right uphill past a square pond, the Bassin du Grand Jet, overlooked by an elegant group of statues. Turn right up steps to follow a path which will bring you to the back of the statues overlooking the Grande Cascade, with a plunging view of the Seine and some well-known Paris landmarks to the left of the skyline in the distance, including the Eiffel Tower and the Sacré-Coeur.

With your back to the statues, go up the steps in front of you, past the rectangular Bassin des Carpes on your right which does not actually contain any carp, as far as I could see. Go up more steps and turn right, past the Bassin des Carpes on your right and continue along the path bordered by a wall up to a small road on the left which leads to the little **Musée Historique** on the right.

This building, formerly the stables, and the larger one opposite, originally servants' and guards' quarters, are the only structures belonging to the château to have survived the fire. The little five-room museum displays the history of the château, and contains a helpful scale model of the original structure.

To the right of the museum there is a discreet entrance to another WC and two vending machines selling coffee, soft drinks and snacks. Or you could make a ten-minute detour to the elegant café **L'Orangerie,** beneath the Jardin de Trocadéro.

Turn left from the museum entrance. The clipped triangular yew trees in front of you mark the outline of the vanished château. Above them to the right is a series of steps which lead up to the **Jardin de Trocadéro**, the high point of the park and of the walk, with spectacular **views** of Paris as you climb.

The plateau at the top of the hill was landscaped around a central lake and a stream in 1823 to create a private garden in which the royal children could study and play, with interior views instead of the formal panoramic views in the rest of the park. It contains rare scented flowering trees from Lebanon and China, chosen to give a continuous display of colour throughout the year. It has been open to the public since 1872, but on weekdays remains a secluded hilltop retreat, with more birds than people. On my recent visit on a sunny Sunday, the park's busiest day, it was full of people picnicking on the grass and watching the ducks but the atmosphere was quiet and peaceful and there was plenty of room for everyone. The grass is dotted with wild flowers.

Go round the lake clockwise to leave the Jardin by the northern corner. Keeping the river on your right and the distinctive church spire of Saint-Cloud in front of you, follow the winding path downhill which will take you past a children's playground on the right to the exit at the Grille des Écoles.

Continue along the path, now called the allée des Lilas, which becomes the rue des Écoles, and passes some picturesque 19th century villas. Continue across the place de Silly, and turn right downhill along the rue Dr Desfossez. This older part of town still feels like a village, with its steep narrow streets clustered around the church. Turn left down steps to go into the side entrance of the 19th-century church, built on the site of a much earlier one. Its spire appears to have been copied from an earlier version, as it is recognisable in the 1675 painting reproduced on p. 129. I have always found it open.

On the left at the back there is a chapel to Saint Clodoald, the grandson of the first French king, Clovis. An elaborate memorial plaque recounts the story of how he escaped the fate of his royal brothers, murdered by their uncles, and grew up to become a priest, renouncing the throne and the world by symbolically cutting off his long hair. He founded a monastery here, which became a place of pilgrimage after his death in 560 and has given the town its name.

His relics are preserved in a casket under the altar of his chapel. The plaque on the left commemorates the visit of the Bishop of Saint-Cloud on the Mississippi to this church in 1922.

Leave the church by the main door next to Saint Clodoald's chapel. To your right is the rue de l'Eglise where further along there is a *boulangerie* selling takeaway coffee, next door to a traditional café. Directly in front of you in place de l'Eglise is a bust of the composer Charles Gounod (1818–1893) who lived in Saint-Cloud, with steps leading down through a little park, the square Gounod, to the tram and bus stops.

Follow the steps down through the park and leave by the exit on the right. Turn right down the busy rue Dailly and cross it at the pedestrian crossing. Look left to find more steps leading down through the rue Audé to the **T2 tram stop Parc de Saint-Cloud.** Trams from here go to Pont de Bezons, stopping at La Défense.

For the **52 and 72 buses** to Paris which terminate here, continue over the footbridge across the tram line and downhill to the bus stops. The terminus for the line 10 **métro, Boulogne Pont de St-Cloud**, is only 500 metres away across the Pont Saint-Cloud, but the walk is so horrible, surrounded by snarling traffic, that I strongly recommend taking either bus there, whichever leaves soonest. Get off two stops later for the métro station, also confusingly known as Rhin et Danube.

The 72 bus ride to Paris is the slowest but by far the most enjoyable route back. Sit on the right-hand side for close-up views of the Eiffel Tower, the Invalides, the Assemblée Nationale, the Musée d'Orsay, the Conciergerie and Notre Dame.

Distance from Paris: 10 km (6 miles)
Depart: Châtelet, métro line 1
Arrive: Pont de Sèvres, métro line 9 (terminus)
Alternative arrival at: Musée de Sèvres, Tram T2
Journey time: 39 minutes
Length of visit: Half or full day
Return from: Parc de Saint-Cloud, terminus for buses 52 or 72
Alternative return from : Parc de Saint-Cloud, Tram T2 or Boulogne Pont de St-Cloud, métro line 10 (terminus)
Navigo Zone: 1
Single ticket: 2.10€
Distance from Pont de Sèvres to Parc de Saint-Cloud: 3½ km (2 miles)
Population (Saint-Cloud): 30,821

Getting there

Métro line 9 Pont de Sèvres and **line 10 Boulogne Pont de St-Cloud** are both about 35 minutes from central Paris and trains run every few minutes. From Châtelet take line 1 to La Défense and change to line 9 at Franklin Roosevelt.

Bus 52 from Parc St-Cloud to Opéra takes about 40 minutes and **bus 72** to Gare de Lyon from Parc St-Cloud takes around 55 minutes to Châtelet. Both buses run approximately every 12 minutes. The **T2 tram** from Parc St-Cloud next to the bus stops takes 13 minutes to La Défense.

Car: D7 along the Left Bank of the Seine to the Musée de Sèvres.

When to go

This accessible short walk with potential shelter in two museums can be done at any time of the year but is at its most enjoyable on a sunny day when the views of Paris are clearest. Note that the Musée de Sèvres is closed at lunchtime and on Tuesdays and the opening hours of the Musée Historique are limited. The park is at its busiest on sunny Sundays but is never uncomfortably crowded. All the fountains and jets are turned on annually every Sunday in June for 25 minutes, at 3, 4 and 5 pm. Free concerts are sometimes held in the park at these times if the weather is fine.

Useful information

Sèvres – Musée National de Céramique, 2 place de la Manufacture Nationale, 92310 Sèvres, tel 01 46 29 22 05, www.sevresciteceramique.fr/en. Open daily except Tuesdays 10 am–1 pm and 2–6 pm. Admission 7€, concessions 5€. Free to everyone on the first Sunday of the month.

Domaine Nationale de Saint-Cloud, www.domaine-saint-cloud.fr. Contains some useful historical and practical information about the château and park, including maps. In French.

Musée Historique de Saint-Cloud, Grille d'Honneur, 92210 Saint-Cloud, tel 01 41 12 02 95, www.domaine-saint-cloud.fr/Actualites/Le-musee-historique-du-domaine-national-de-Saint-Cloud. Open Wednesday 3 pm–6 pm, 3.30–7 pm between May and August, and on certain weekends at the same times. Admission free.

Cafés

L'Orangerie, Bassin des 24 Jets, Parc Saint-Cloud, tel 09 86 43 95 75, www.lorangerie24jets.com. Open in theory 10 am-6 pm daily, but opening hours may be dependent on the weather.

Café-tabac de la Colline, 37 rue d'Orléans, Saint-Cloud, tel 01 46 02 10 46. Open daily to 8.30 pm except Sundays, when it closes at 1 pm.

10. Parc de Bagatelle

An exclusive Arcadia of irises, roses, waterfalls and peacocks on the edge of Paris

The diminutive château de Bagatelle (a *bagatelle* is an airy nothing, a trifle) is in an enclosed park within the Bois de Boulogne, on the western edge of Paris, accessible by métro, bus and a short walk. The park is famous for its roses but I make a point of going there when the iris garden is in flower for about three weeks between mid May and early June, as it is then that it offers maximum *dépaysement* (change of scene). There are 330 varieties of iris represented in a brief explosion of every conceivable colour and form, in a hidden garden at the edge of the park.

The park covers only 25 hectares, but feels larger because of the artfully arranged nooks and crannies it contains. It is not well-known to foreign visitors and you can find quiet corners even on sunny Sundays in summer. You can sit on the grass which is scattered with wild flowers and spring bulbs *à l'anglaise*, so you will see tulips growing next to bluebells, daisies and cowslips. The sight and sound of water are never far away. The park contains exotic flowers and trees, several follies, lakes with water-lilies, grottoes with stepping stones, waterfalls, little bridges, hidden arbours, and flaunting peacocks wherever you go. Their hoarse calls echo periodically across the quiet park and they are capable of strutting up to you and gazing soulfully into your face if you happen to be eating anything. The ducks are equally tame and the less-visited eastern fringe near the *buvette* is home to some stray cats who are wary but tolerant of humans.

The large terrace of the upmarket restaurant to the right of the main entrance is the best place from which to watch the elegant inhabitants of the 16th *arrondissement* of Paris in which the park is situated. The *buvette* is quieter, more modestly priced and more relaxed.

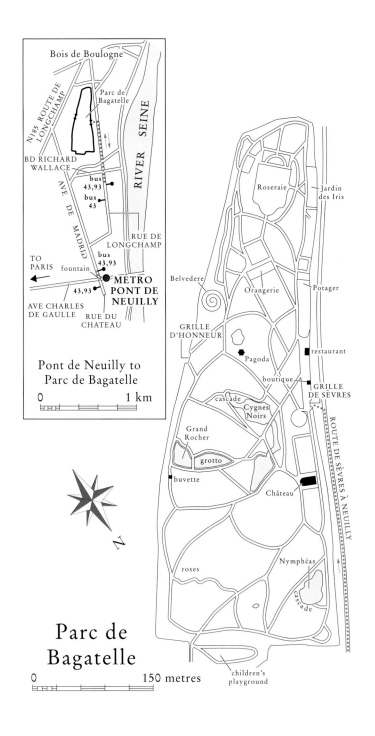

Bois de Boulogne

Parc de Bagatelle

N185 ROUTE DE LONGCHAMP

RIVER SEINE

BD RICHARD WALLACE

AVE. DE MADRID

bus 43,93

bus 43

RUE DE LONGCHAMP

TO PARIS

fountain

bus 43,93

43,93

METRO PONT DE NEUILLY

AVE CHARLES DE GAULLE

RUE DU CHATEAU

Pont de Neuilly to Parc de Bagatelle

0   1 km

N

Roseraie

Jardin des Iris

Belvedere

Orangerie

Potager

GRILLE D'HONNEUR

Pagoda

restaurant

boutique

GRILLE DE SÈVRES

cascade

Cygnes Noirs

ROUTE DE SÈVRES À NEUILLY

Grand Rocher

grotto

buvette

Château

roses

Nymphéas

cascade

Parc de Bagatelle

0   150 metres

children's playground

The château de Bagatelle

The château was built in just 64 days in 1777 for a bet between Marie-Antoinette and her brother-in-law, the Comte d'Artois, later Charles X. He won the bet, at a cost which was rather more than a trifle. The park was designed in a single night in the fashionable Anglo-Chinese style, with a pagoda, a 'ruined' abbey, lakes, waterfalls and grottoes artfully imitating nature. The domain was later the home of the reclusive and fabulously wealthy English collector, the fourth Marquess of Hertford, and then of his son Sir Richard Wallace, the creator of the graceful green Wallace fountains in Paris, and founder of the Wallace Collection in London. The estate was saved from dismemberment by the City of Paris, who bought it in 1905. It is now one of the city's four botanic gardens.

Suggested visit to the Parc de Bagatelle

Take 'Sortie 2, avenue de Madrid' from the **Pont de Neuilly métro**. With your back to the square arch at La Défense take the first street on the right with the Crédit Lyonnais bank on the corner, the avenue de Madrid. The **'Pont de Neuilly' bus stop** for the 43 to Neuilly Bagatelle and the 93 to Suresnes is a few steps after the bank, on the same side of the road. Take either bus and get off four stops later at 'Place de Bagatelle'.

There is a *boulangerie* with tables outside just behind the bus stop in the place de Bagatelle, on the corner of the rue de Longchamp and the rue Ernest Deloison. It is open all year round and a good place to stop for coffee and pastries. There is a small supermarket opposite where you can buy picnic supplies, open to 1.30 pm on Sundays.

Continue down the rue de Longchamp in the direction taken by the bus and you will see the Bois de Boulogne ahead of you. Cross the boulevard Richard Wallace at the traffic lights into the Bois, where you will see a sign on the right, 'Parc de Bagatelle'. Take the footpath which you will eventually see on the left-hand side of the road and continue for half a kilometre

Château de Bagatelle

until you come to the Grille de Sèvres entrance to the **Parc de Bagatelle**.

From here turn sharp right, past the boutique, *les toilettes* and the **restaurant**, and on through a long narrow garden planted with arbours of wisteria, with roses and clematis climbing the wall on your right. Go straight on and through the next garden which becomes a *jardin potager* (kitchen garden, where I filched a raspberry), then past a bamboo grove at the end.

The **Jardin des Iris** lies just beyond this, slightly hidden, with the entrance on the right. There are benches at the less visited far end in front of a little fountain, an idyllic place in which to picnic. When I bent down to sniff the irises one crowded sunny Sunday in May (each colour has a slightly different smell) all the elegant *seizième* old ladies started doing the same. *Seizième* just means 'sixteenth' but to Parisians is a loaded adjective, evoking the old wealth traditionally associated with this *arrondissement*.

The *Roseraie* for which Bagatelle is famous is opposite the iris garden but to my mind not as unusual or rewarding, although of course a rose is always a rose, and there are around ten thousand of them, representing 1,200 species. Go through it and towards the Orangerie on your left. At this point you could veer left to return to the entrance and the château nearby, but it is well worth following the map for a rewarding ramble in the park.

I particularly recommend the **Grotte Cascade Pièce d'Eau des Cygnes Noirs** ('grotto and waterfall at the lake of black swans') for its dramatic water effects and the quiet *buvette* with its elegant wooden furniture shaded by green parasols near the 'Grand Rocher' where you can order a beer or a coffee to accompany your picnic, and perhaps share it with the peacocks and the ducks. It is also well worth a detour to the **Cascade Pièce d'Eau des Nymphéas** ('waterfall at the water-lily lake') for the pleasure of using the stepping stones across the water to sit in a 'secret' rocky grotto, watching the ducks and coots and an occasional heron. You can see the little **château de Bagatelle** from here, not far from the park entrance. It cannot be visited but you can peep through the windows to admire the 18th century furnishings. It has the Latin words *Parva sed apta* carved over the front ('small but appropriate').

Cascade des Nymphéas

Leave the park by the entrance you came in by and return to the place de Bagatelle bus stop on the right hand side of the road for the 43 bus back to the Pont de Neuilly, from where you can take the métro. If you decide to stay on the bus for a slower but more visually rewarding return to Paris, the 43 ends at the Gare du Nord.

If you prefer to walk to the métro, it is 1½ km from the bus stop, following the quiet rue de Longchamp all the way and turning right at the end. You will pass the former house of the writer Théophile Gautier at no. 32, next to an old sign forbidding people from letting their horses and oxen mount the pavement. The street after this point feels like a slightly theatrical but charming village, with a sprinkling of upmarket restaurants, cafés and local shops.

Distance from Paris: 10½ km (6½ miles)
Depart: Châtelet, Métro Line 1
Arrive: Pont de Neuilly métro, then bus to place de Bagatelle
Journey time:
around 32 minutes, 22 by métro and 10 by bus
Length of visit: Half or full day
Navigo Zone: 2
Single ticket: 2.10€
Distance from place de Bagatelle to Parc de Bagatelle: ½ km (546 yards)
Distance from place de Bagatelle to Pont de Neuilly métro: 1½ km (1 mile)

Getting there

Take **Métro Line 1 to Pont de Neuilly** and then **bus 43** or **93** from the Pont de Neuilly bus stop. Both buses run daily, approximately every 10 minutes up to around midnight. You can use your Navigo or a Paris métro ticket in these buses.

Car: N185 towards Route de Sèvres à Neuilly

RATP maps *no. 2* (Paris) or *plan de secteur, no. 5*. See p. 179.

When to go

You will see flowers in the park during every month of the year except December, but the most rewarding displays are in spring and summer. The irises are in flower for about three weeks between mid-May and early June, and the roses from May to November.

Useful information

Parc de Bagatelle, route de Sèvres à Neuilly, Bois de Boulogne, 75016 Paris, tel 01 53 64 53 80. http://en.parisinfo.com/paris-museum-monument/71636/Parc-de-Bagatelle in English, https://www.paris.fr/equipements/parc-de-bagatelle-1808 in French. You can download the park map from the French website. Open daily to 8 pm in spring and summer, 5 pm in winter. From April to September admission is 2.50€, free the rest of the year.

http://www.perso-jardins-bagatelle.net/indexenglish.htm is an unofficial website with lovely photos and additional information, some of it in English, and a clickable map.

Restaurants and cafés

Les Jardins de Bagatelle restaurant, Parc de Bagatelle, tel 01 40 67 98 29, http://bagatellelerestaurant.fr/restaurant/. Open daily from 11.30 am to around 3.30 pm. Large terrace, crowded with elegant locals when the weather is fine. Rather minuscule main dishes at around 25€, but you can order just a glass of wine at 7€ or coffee at 3.50€.

The upmarket *buvette* sells ices, *crêpes*, beer, tea and coffee and is located in a quieter part of the park, suitable for a picnic.

11. Malmaison

A unique glimpse into the private lives of Napoleon and Josephine at the château de Malmaison. Optional stroll through the park for lunch in the historic centre of Rueil opposite the church where Josephine is buried and riverside walk to Rueil-Malmaison

The elegant little château de Malmaison is in a lovely setting within easy reach of Paris, which is why Napoleon and Josephine chose it, but has few international visitors. You could enjoyably prolong this trip by taking a short walk through the Parc de Bois-Préau next door, which once belonged to the château, to the church where Josephine is buried in the historic centre of Rueil. It is an attractive little town with a market and a good brasserie next to the church. You could end the trip with a short bus ride to Bougival to take a beautiful 3 km walk back along the Seine at a spot made famous by the Impressionists, past the house of Georges Bizet to the station at Rueil-Malmaison.

Napoleon and Josephine at Malmaison

The more you know about Napoleon and Josephine, the more rewarding the visit will be. These two highly successful self-made people had a lot in common and each died with the other's name on their lips. Josephine de Beauharnais was a 32-year old widow with two children, from a minor aristocratic family in Martinique, living on her beauty and her wits in the precarious world of the Directory which governed France from 1795 to 1799. She was six years older than the rising but socially unpolished young general when he met and fell in love with her. They married a few months later in 1796 despite the opposition of his family, who felt that he could have done much better. It seems that she was not in love

Château de Malmaison

with him and that Napoleon was furious when he found out about at least one lover soon after their marriage. He turned out to be a devoted step-father to Josephine's children and all the evidence is that she eventually fell deeply in love with him. The divorce in 1809 was reluctantly arranged so that he could marry again when it was clear that she could not provide the Emperor with an heir. He made a generous settlement on her, including Malmaison and its valuable contents, insisted that she keep the title of Empress, and continued to support her financially despite her extravagance. He once remarked that the only thing that ever came between them was her debts. They stayed good friends until her death at Malmaison, aged 51, in 1814. After his abdication on 22 June 1815 Napoleon spent a few days at Malmaison before leaving France for exile on St Helena.

The 17th-century château was acquired by Josephine in 1799 and Napoleon paid for it on his return from Egypt. He employed two young architects, Percier and Fontaine, to do major renovation work on it between 1800 and 1802 although he curtailed their more ambitious plans to remodel it completely. Unlike Rambouillet and St-Cloud, former royal châteaux which

François Gérard, The Empress Josephine, c. 1808

became Napoleon's later residences, Malmaison was redesigned as a private country house where the First Consul could entertain, work and relax. Between 1800 and 1802 the government known as the Consulate (1799-1804), of which Napoleon was the leading member, met there frequently, in a more informal atmosphere than that of the Tuileries.

Josephine's pioneering but expensive tastes were expressed most fully in the vast park of 726 hectares, which at one point included a menagerie of exotic animals, until Napoleon decreed that they had to go. Her lifelong interest was botany and the hothouses at Malmaison were filled with at least 200 plants unknown in France before then, dahlias, lilies and particularly roses, of which there were more than 250 varieties by 1814. She employed an English landscape gardener and kept up a correspondence with the director of Kew Gardens. During the war both the French and English Admiralties colluded to allow ships carrying rare plants for Malmaison through the blockade and the beautiful flower paintings of her illustrator, Redouté, made his name. After the divorce, her chief interest, after her grand-children, was her plants. It was Josephine who pioneered the modern hybridisation of roses and the use of vernacular rather than Latin names for them. She was also the first person in Europe to successfully rear black swans in captivity, brought from Tasmania in 1802. They have been re-introduced into the park.

Suggested visit to the château de Malmaison

From **La Défense/Grande Arche station** follow the exit signs for the bus terminal inside the RER station and the **258 bus** to La Jonchère. Get off about 25 minutes later at 'Le château', having pressed the red button beforehand to stop the bus if someone else hasn't already done so.

Cross the road, turn left and then first right down the quiet tree-lined avenue du château de Malmaison which leads to the **château**, 300 metres away on the right.

Napoleon and Josephine had the château redesigned and furnished in the fashionably simple yet elevated classical style of the Consulate, to which it has been carefully restored, right down to the striped silk curtains in the Salle de Conseil, recall-ing a military tent. The dignified half columns outside, support-ing classical statues, were actually props needed to prevent the structure from collapsing while the house was being aggrandised for its new role as home to the First Consul and his wife, ef-fectively the First Lady. The black and white flooring on the ground floor was cleverly designed to unify the entrance hall, dining room and billiard room, which became one vast ballroom when the doors were swung back. The dining room frescoes of dancing girls in the Pompeian style recall Napoleon's later rooms at Rambouillet, as do the Egyptian motifs. The portraits of Josephine reveal her elegance and her undisputed role as an arbiter of fashion. Like many other people at that time, she had decayed teeth and was always painted with her mouth closed, lips slightly curved in a mysterious smile.

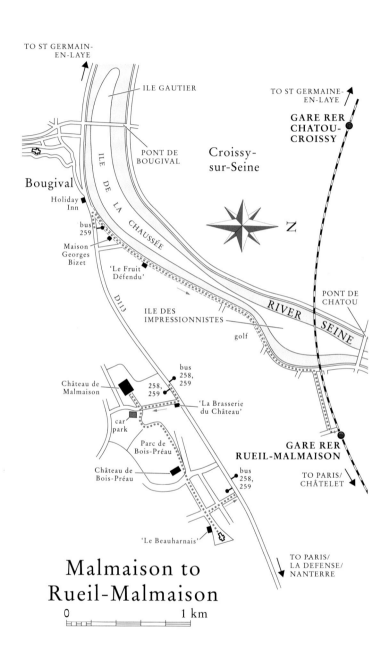

TO ST GERMAIN-
EN-LAYE

ILE GAUTIER

TO ST GERMAINE-
EN-LAYE

GARE RER
CHATOU-
CROISSY

PONT DE
BOUGIVAL

Croissy-
sur-Seine

Bougival

Holiday
Inn

N

bus
259

Maison
Georges
Bizet

'Le Fruit
Défendu'

ILE DE LA CHAUSSÉE

D113

PONT DE
CHATOU

ILE DES
IMPRESSIONNISTES

golf

RIVER SEINE

Château de
Malmaison

bus
258,
259

258,
259

'La Brasserie
du Château'

car
park

GARE RER
RUEIL-MALMAISON

Parc de
Bois-Préau

Château de
Bois-Préau

bus
258,
259

TO PARIS/
CHÂTELET

'Le Beauharnais'

TO PARIS/
LA DEFENSE/
NANTERRE

Malmaison to
Rueil-Malmaison

0   1 km

The **park** contains a magnificent cedar of Lebanon, now higher than the château, planted by Napoleon and Josephine in 1800, the year of the victory of Marengo. Although reduced to a tiny fraction of its original size, the park is pretty and quiet, landscaped *à l'anglaise* with a stream and a little bridge from which you can watch the black swans. In summer you can sniff some of the roses for which Malmaison became famous, including the beautiful sweetly-scented *Souvenir de Joséphine*.

There is no tea room at the château and you are not supposed to picnic in the grounds, so the **Brasserie du Château**, on your right at the end of the avenue du Château on the way back is your nearest option for food. From there turn left onto the main road for the 258 bus stop 'Le château' going back to **La Défense** or you could take the 259 bus from the same stop to **Nanterre Préfecture RER station** if it comes first, getting off at the 'Esplanade Charles de Gaulle' stop. Both bus journeys take around 20 minutes.

However, I have found it much more rewarding to take the pretty walk through the Parc de Bois-Préau next to the château to the church in the heart of the historic centre of Rueil, where Josephine is buried. There is a better, more authentic brasserie with a traffic-free terrace facing the church in the main square and it is a short walk from there through the attractive little town and its market place to the next bus stop.

Optional 1½ km walk through the Parc de Bois-Préau to Rueil

From the château entrance take the pedestrian crossing to your right and go into the car-park. Turn left to eventually join a little footpath sign-posted **'Parc de Bois-Préau'** (pronounced Pray-oh). Go through an opening in the wall ahead and turn left to follow the yellow PR sign (see pp. 177-178) for the path into the park. Turn left, past *les toilettes*, and continue along the main path for almost a kilometre, following the signs for 'Centre-Ville'.

The park belonged to the **château de Bois-Préau**, which you will eventually pass, and was landscaped *à l'anglaise* in the 18th century. It is now open to the public but has kept its original

Château de Bois-Préau and statue of Josephine

appearance, offering wide vistas, a little stream, and some stately old trees, dotted with occasional statues and benches and
roamed by a flock of Canada geese. I have found drifts of snowdrops growing here in January. Josephine tried several times to
buy it so that she could extend the park from Malmaison but her
neighbour resolutely refused to sell and the Empress had to wait
until the owner's death before she was able to acquire the property in 1810. There is a statue of her in coronation robes in front
of the château, which you will pass on your right. The château,
like the park, has become an extension of Malmaison, housing
a museum dedicated to Napoleon's exile, death and continuing
legend. It is currently closed for renovation.

Leave the park at the exit just after the château and cross the
road on your right to continue straight ahead into the small semi-
pedestrianised rue Jean Le Coz , lined with 18th and 19th century
houses. Follow it to the end, passing the **Office de Tourisme** on
your right. You will see the baroque façade of the **Eglise de St
Pierre et St Paul** framed between the buildings at the end of the
street.

The church contains Josephine's tomb surmounted by
a statue of her kneeling, in the same pose as at her coronation.
Her tomb faces the mausoleum of her daughter, Hortense de
Beauharnais, step-daughter of Napoleon, wife of his younger
brother, and mother of Napoleon III, who paid for the resto-

ration of his mother's monument in 1858. Although part of it dates back to the 12th century, the church feels very much like a Bonaparte family chapel and it is always open.

There is a well-established brasserie in the place de l'Eglise with a large outside terrace, shaded in summer and heated in winter, aptly called **Le Beauharnais**. It is a good place in which to sit and savour the relaxed, almost provincial atmosphere of the little town. I have only shared a *planche mixte* here, a generous platter of cheese and charcuterie, but the menu includes classic French dishes as well as snacks and vegetarian options. My friendly neighbours at the next table confirmed that the place is deservedly popular with the locals.

Return to the end of the rue Jean Le Coz and turn right to continue in a straight line down the semi-pedestrianised rue Hervet, over the Boulevard de Maréchal Foch, through place Jean Jaurès where the **market** is held, and along rue de la Réunion, which ends back at the main bus route, avenue Paul Doumer. Turn left for the 'Danielle Casanova' stop for buses 258 and 259 towards Paris.

To continue to Bougival for the riverside walk 3 km away, cross the road and turn left for the 259 bus stop towards St Germain-en-Laye.

Optional 3 km riverside walk from Bougival to Rueil-Malmaison

This part of Bougival with its pastoral views of the Seine was a favourite with artists and writers in the 19th century and has changed very little. See p. 164 for more information about Bougival's popularity with artists. Get off the bus about 10 minutes and seven stops later at 'La Chaussée–Musée Tourgueniev', and continue walking for a few metres in the direction of the bus until you see the start of the footpath by the Seine. There is a reproduction here of Monet's atmospheric 1867 painting of the Seine at Bougival in winter.

Turn right to follow the riverside path which leads past some 19th century villas. You will soon pass the tall house briefly

The Seine at Bougival

rented by **Georges Bizet** (1838-1875) in which he worked furiously to finish *Carmen*, an opera which initially shocked the public and critics alike. He died there of an aneurysm at the age of 36, three months after its disastrous première. There is a small plaque put up in 1912 but it is easy to miss unless you are walking in the opposite direction.

You will eventually pass a tennis club with a garden and a cosy **bar** furnished with a log fire and armchairs, open to the public as well as club members. **'Le Fruit Défendu'** (Forbidden Fruit) next door is an upmarket riverside restaurant, part of the same establishment.

Continue along the river, passing a pony club and a golf course en route, until you see a railway bridge ahead with a sign for the RER, with some huge barges moored nearby. Turn right along the avenue de la Seine, following the railway line overhead on your left. At the end of the avenue turn left to find steps leading up to a handy footbridge over the busy main road, taking you straight to the entrance to **Rueil-Malmaison station**.

Distance from Paris: 15 km
(9 miles)
Depart: 258 bus from La
Défense/Grande Arche station
(RER A and Métro Line 1)
Arrive: 'Le château' bus stop
Journey time:
25 minutes or less
Length of visit: Half or full day
Alternative return from:
RER A Nanterre Préfecture or
Rueil-Malmaison
Navigo Zone: 3
Single ticket: 2.10€ (3.10€
from Nanterre Préfecture,
4.05€ from Rueil-Malmaison)
**Distance from château de
Malmaison to Rueil via Parc
de Bois-Préau:** 1.5 km (1 mile)
**Distance from Rueil to
Bougival :** 3 km (2 miles)
**Distance from Bougival to
Rueil-Malmaison station:** 3 km
(2 miles)
Population: Rueil-Malmaison,
76,909

Getting there

The **258 bus** from La Défense to
La Jonchère runs daily at 10-20
minute intervals, up to midnight.

NB: La Défense/Grande
Arche is in Zone 3, so if you travel
there by RER you will need to
buy a ticket for that destination. If
you go there by Métro Line 1 you
can use an ordinary Paris métro
ticket. You can also use a Paris
métro ticket on the 258 and 259
buses. It is slightly more expensive
to buy a ticket from the driver.

If you return from Nanterre
Préfecture station **RER A trains**

run every 15 minutes up to about
midnight, taking 20 minutes or
less to Châtelet-Les Halles. The
journey from Rueil-Malmaison
takes 25 minutes. The **259 bus** between St-Germain-en-Laye and
Nanterre Anatole France runs at
the same frequency as the 258 and
takes 21 minutes from 'Le château'
stop to Nanterre Préfecture.

Car: RN 13 tunnel exit from
La Défense, towards St Germain-
en-Laye.

RATP map *plan de secteur,
no. 5* is very useful. See p. 179.

When to go

Sunny weather in spring or summer is preferable if you want to
see the château and the roses in
the park at their best, but you
could go at any time of the year.
The château is closed on Tuesdays
and between 12.30 and 1.30 pm.
The Parc de Bois-Préau is also
closed on Tuesdays. The market
is held on Tuesday and Saturday
mornings up to 1 pm.

The château can get crowded
in the afternoon on summer
weekends, so I would recommend
arriving at around 11 am. The
gates close at noon but you can
wander in the park while the château is closed at lunchtime, as the
caretaker will let you out.

Useful information

Château de Malmaison, avenue
du château de Malmaison, 92500
Rueil Malmaison, tel 01 41 29

05 55, http://musees-nationaux-malmaison.fr. Open daily, except Tuesdays, 25 December and 1 January: 10 am–12.30 pm and 1.30–5.15 pm in winter, 5.45 pm at weekends. In summer open to 5.45 pm, 6.15 pm at weekends. The park is open 10 am–6 pm, 6.30 pm in summer. Last admission in the morning is at noon, when the gates close. Admission 6.50€, concessions 5€, free to EU residents under 26 and to everyone on the first Sunday of the month. Admission to the park only, 1.50€.

Office de Tourisme de Rueil-Malmaison, 33 rue Jean le Coz, tel 01 47 32 35 75, www.rueil-tourisme.com/en. Open Monday-Friday 10 am–12.30 pm and 1.30–6 pm. Their website contains a useful downloadable tourist brochure and map (in French).

Restaurants

La Brasserie du Château, 193 avenue Napoléon Bonaparte, 92500 Rueil-Malmaison, tel 01 47 51 82 83, www.brasserie-du-chateau.com. Open Tuesday to Saturday and up to 2.30 pm on Sunday, closed in August. Garden. Two-course *formule* at 35€, three-course menu 42€. Traditional French cooking and seafood specialities but few à la carte or vegetarian options. Wine from 4.50€ a glass.

Le Beauharnais brasserie, 29 place de l'Eglise, tel 01 41 29 12 21. Open daily. A la carte only. Traditional dishes such as *cochon de lait* (roast sucking pig) around 20€, vegetarian and snack options, 50 cl *pichet* of wine from 17€ or from 4.50€ a glass.

12. Marly-le-Roi

A rewarding stroll from Marly-le-Roi and Louveciennes to the Seine at Bougival, in the footsteps of the Roi Soleil and the Impressionists

I found this 4½ km walk, adapted from the tourist office walk 'Pays des Impressionistes', to be surprisingly good value. I had never heard of Louveciennes until it was mentioned to me by a French friend, and had always thought of the western suburbs of Paris as boringly residential. But in the event I was charmed by the old villages at the heart of these prosperous suburbs, intrigued by the 17th century Parc de Marly, the aqueduct at Louveciennes and the Machine de Marly, and delighted by the dramatic descent from the wooded hill at Louveciennes to the Seine at Bougival. So were the Impressionist painters, some of whose canvases are reproduced at the viewpoints where they were painted along the route.

The walk is a voyage of discovery of aspects of French history not known to many visitors. It can be shortened by a return from the station at Louveciennes or prolonged by a 2 km detour to the old village of Bougival.

The Château de Marly

Marly-le-Roi owes its name to the creation of the Château de Marly there for Louis XIV by Jules Hardouin-Mansart in 1686. It was designed as a country retreat from where the king could hunt and entertain a select number of friends in a less formal setting than that of Versailles, from which all the game had fled. 'J'ai fait Versailles pour ma cour, Trianon pour ma famille, Marly pour mes amis' ('I created Versailles for my court, Trianon for my family and Marly for my friends') was how he put it.

Grande Rue, Marly-le-Roi

An invitation to Marly was the highest mark of the king's favour. The château was constructed to reflect this, in the form of a zodiac with the Sun King's pavilion in the middle surrounded by twelve pavilions for his guests. Its waterfall, the Grande Cascade, was supplied by water pumped uphill by the famous Machine de Marly from the Seine at Bougival two kilometres away and transported by the aqueduct Mansart constructed at Louveciennes. Inaugurated in 1684, the Machine was a complicated series of vast and extremely noisy pumps designed to supply the fountains of Versailles as well as those of Marly, a unique feat of engineering described at the time as 'the Eighth Wonder of the World'. The Grande Cascade at Marly, ruinously expensive to run, was replaced by the Tapis Vert (Green Carpet) after the king's death and the château itself was demolished in the 19th century.

Today Marly-le-Roi is a prosperous residential suburb of Paris, but the atmosphere of the Grand Siècle of Louis XIV still lingers in the old village at its heart and the château park. It is tangibly present in the aqueduct which is still standing and in the remains of the Machine de Marly at Bougival, a spot which became an inspiration to painters in the 19th century.

The neighbouring village of Louveciennes soon developed into a courtly residential overspill of Marly. In the 18th century the long residence there of Madame du Barry, the last mistress of Louis XV, in the house formerly occupied by the Governor of the Machine de Marly, gave it a lustre which attracted artists: her friend, the painter Elisabeth Vigée-Lebrun, the poets André Chénier and Leconte de Lisle, and in the 20th century the sculptor Aristide Maillol, the American writer Anaïs Nin and the German composer Kurt Weill. But it is above all the 19th century Impressionist painters, Renoir, Sisley and Pissarro, who have familiarised the world with the charm of the local landscapes, even though few people have visited the actual spots where they were painted.

2.4 km walk from Marly-le-Roi station to Louveciennes church

Leave by the main station exit and take the tree-lined slightly uphill road opposite, the avenue du Général Leclerc. Continue uphill over the little roundabout and straight on into the rue Alexandre Dumas, with a stately church visible ahead. This cobbled street leads to the heart of the old village of Marly, with the Grande Rue, its main street, downhill on the left. Continue to the end of the rue Alexandre Dumas and cross the road to the **Eglise de St Vigor**.

Louis XIV had it built by Mansart in 1689 at the request of the villagers, to replace the two crumbling churches of the former parishes of Marly-le-Chastel and Marly-le-Bourg, which then became known as Marly-le-Roi. The only church Mansart ever built, it is impressive for its elegance rather than for its religious atmosphere. A painting on the left which appears to be of the Virgin and child is of Saint Frances of Rome, often depicted holding the Christ child, with the face of Madame de Maintenon.

On leaving the church turn left and cross the road to look

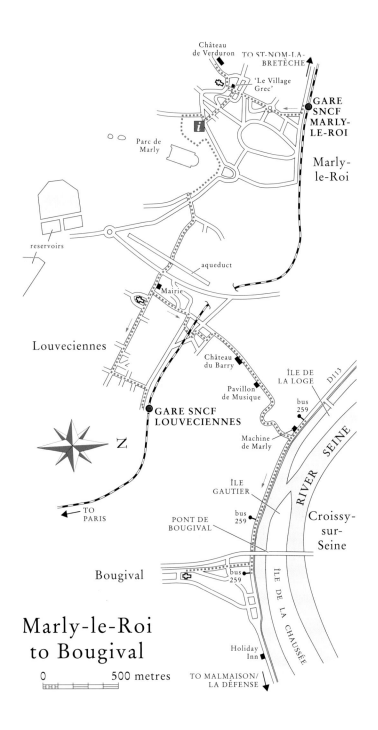

Château de Verduron

TO ST-NOM-LA-BRETÈCHE

'Le Village Grec'

GARE SNCF MARLY-LE-ROI

i

Parc de Marly

Marly-le-Roi

reservoirs

aqueduct

Mairie

Louveciennes

Château du Barry

ÎLE DE LA LOGE

D113

Pavillon de Musique

bus 259

GARE SNCF LOUVECIENNES

Machine de Marly

Z

ÎLE GAUTIER

RIVER SEINE

bus 259

Croissy-sur-Seine

TO PARIS

PONT DE BOUGIVAL

bus 259

Bougival

bus 259

ÎLE DE LA CHAUSSÉE

Holiday Inn

TO MALMAISON/LA DÉFENSE

Marly-le-Roi
to Bougival

0   500 metres

through the gates of the **Château de Verduron** at the incongruous double row of sphinxes lining the approach to the hidden
château. Like many other buildings in Marly, it was constructed
for one of the courtiers of Louis XIV. In 1863 it became the home
of the popular playwright Victorien Sardou (1831–1908), author
of *La Tosca*, who installed the sphinxes, originally designed by
the distinguished Egyptologist Auguste Mariette for the Egyptian
pavilion of the 1867 *Exposition Universelle*.

Return downhill to the rue Alexandre Dumas, past **Le
Village Grec** on your left (see p. 167). Continue down the narrow, slightly crooked Grande Rue on your right. Although lined
with some rather twee shops and modish restaurants, it still feels
like an old village street. Towards the end on the right, the café-
tabac **Le Narval** with tables outside, popular with the locals, is
a good place to stop for a drink or a snack. You can also buy
sandwiches here to take away. There is no *boulangerie* nearby.

Continue to the end of the Grande Rue and cross the main
road, the avenue des Combattants, to the **tourist office** opposite. With your back to the tourist office, turn left and continue
uphill for the entrance to the **Parc de Marly** on your left, an
ordered 17th-century world of quiet green avenues. The only
sound when I was there was of chestnuts softly falling around us.

Follow the small road through the park straight on for
about 30 metres and then take the first path on your left, and
continue across an avenue of lime trees towards Le Grand
Miroir, a rectangular stretch of water bordered by formal cone-
shaped clipped hedges (see p. 31). It is a popular place for pic-
nics. Continue left, skirting the water, to find the blue and gold
railings of the terrace overlooking the Abreuvoir, a horseshoe-
shaped pond at the edge of the park facing the Le Grand Miroir.
It was a spot particularly favoured by Sisley, who lived nearby.
The view is framed by the famous **Chevaux de Marly** at each
side, two strikingly realistic sculptures of a rearing horse being
hauled into submission by a naked would-be rider, commis-
sioned by Louis XV in 1739 (see p. 26). The originals are in the
Cour de Marly in the Louvre.

From the Abreuvoir there is a **view** of a green slope in the
distance rising behind Le Grand Miroir, the Tapis Vert, giving

you an idea of the scale of the vanished Grande Cascade and the quantities of water that must have been required for it. With your back to the Abreuvoir turn left, past one of the sculpted horses, and take the path on the edge of the park uphill, past a reproduction of one of Sisley's many paintings of the Abreuvoir, until you come to an old wooden doorway set into a massive stone arch, the Porte du Cœur Volant (see p. 22). Go through the doorway and cross the road to go straight on along the chemin du Cœur Volant opposite, a small slightly uphill road signed 'Louveciennes-Centre'.

Take the first turning on the right into the chemin de l'Aqueduc, which winds uphill. You will soon see the arcades of the huge **aqueduct** at Louveciennes ahead, constructed in 1685. Its 36 arcades are still standing and it was in use until 1866, when it was replaced by an underground hydraulic system.

When you get to the aqueduct, cross the grass to its other side, where there are two benches. This is an ideal place for a picnic, with a hilltop **view** over Louveciennes, its church spire visible above the trees and the unexpected sight of a sunny vineyard directly in front of you (see cover photo). It is run by a local association producing small quantities of a wine called Les Côteaux de Louveciennes, unfortunately not for sale. There are some well-executed graffitti carved into the walls of the aqueduct here, dating from 1843 onwards.

Follow the chemin de l'Aqueduc downhill and cross the busy main road, the Route de Versailles, at the traffic lights. Continue straight on, down the quiet little rue du Général Leclerc opposite, where you will see the church at Louveciennes coming into view. Continue towards the church, passing the 18th century building housing the Mairie on the left which has a towering sequoia tree in front of it. The Café de la Mairie on the right is closed on Sundays but the quiet **Eglise St Martin et St Blaise**, built between the 11th and 14th centuries, is always open. It is well worth a visit for its stained glass windows which glow like jewels in the dark interior, and two curiously elongated unnamed medieval statues of a king and a queen near the altar. Notice the quaint carved faces over the main porch of the church, which is now accessed by the side entrance.

You now have the choice of returning to Paris from the nearby **station at Louveciennes** or of continuing to the River Seine and taking a bus and train back to Paris. I recommend the chemin de la Machine and the scenic descent to the Seine at Bougival as the high point of the walk in every sense, but be aware that the footpath down the hill is fairly steep and can be slippery in wet weather, although there is a handrail.

Alternative 1 km walk from the church to Louveciennes station

Continue past the church along the rue Général Leclerc. On the left at no. 10, just after the junction with the rue de la Croix Rouge, there is a plaque to **Elisabeth Vigée-Lebrun**, whose country house stood on the spot now occupied by the Résidence Dauphine block of flats next door. She lived there from 1809 to 1842, and has left a vivid description of the entrance of three Prussian soldiers, sabres in hand, into her bedroom at 11 pm 'on a night I shall never forget', that of 31st March 1814. She lay in bed trembling while they prodded the covers for hidden money, despite the expostulations of her Swiss manservant who spoke German, and then ransacked the house for four terrible hours before leaving.

Further on, tucked into a corner of the street after the impasse Carnot on the left, you will see an attractive house with a plaque informing you that it was **Renoir**'s studio between 1897 and 1914. Continue along the winding rue Leclerc uphill, turning left, past the rue Auguste Renoir on your right, and downhill into the rue de Montbuisson. On your right at no. 2 *bis* is another plaque commemorating **Anaïs Nin**, who lived here between 1931 and 1935. At the end of the rue Montbuisson turn right for the **station** at Louveciennes. Stay on the right and just before crossing the road to the station you will see a reproduction of the scene in 1870 painted by Pissarro. The aqueduct crowning the hill in the painting is still visible in the distance on your left.

2 km walk from the church to the Machine de Marly at Bougival

On leaving the church return to the Mairie and turn right into the residential rue de la Paix. Continue for some way until you come to the second turning on the left, where the road forks. Take the right hand fork, the rue de la Grande Fontaine, and then the first left to follow it through the tunnel under the railway line. Take the first left and then the first right, rue Traversière. Turn left uphill into the rue de la Princesse and then first right to enter the **chemin de la Machine**, a peaceful broad avenue bordered by chestnut and lime trees.

The right-hand side of the whole street was once occupied by the Pavillon des Eaux, a property constructed in 1684 for the governor of the Machine de Marly and enlarged in 1769 for Madame du Barry, so it is confusingly also known as the **château de Madame du Barry**. She was arrested there in 1793 and died on the guillotine three months later.

On the left you will see a reproduction of a Sisley painting showing this spot, still easily recognisable. After the **Pavillon des Eaux** you will pass the Pavillon de Musique, a neo-classical extension of the château added by Madame du Barry in 1771. It originally overlooked the steep hill at the end of the road with a plunging view of the Seine but the whole building was moved to its present position in 1923 by its then owner, the perfumer François Coty, because of the risk of subsidence.

At the end of the road take the footpath winding steeply down through the wooded hillside. Various faded notices en route explain the history of the Machine de Marly, in extremely technical detail, and there is a **viewing table** to help you identify landmarks in the valley of the Seine stretching out in front of you (see photograph p. 41). You can see the river sparkling below and the office tower blocks of La Défense in the distance. On the way down you will pass a reproduction of Sisley's painting of the view from here in 1873, with a farmhouse in the foreground. The farmhouse was originally a forge used in the construction of the Machine and its ruins have only recently been demolished.

At the end of the path you will see the river ahead of you

Le chemin de la Machine, Louveciennes, Alfred Sisley, 1873

and steps down to the main road. You will pass the 17th-century house of the Machine's first superintendent, Joachim Cochu, on the right, which has been restored and converted into flats. Turn left onto the busy D113 to find the site of the **Machine de Marly**, at the Pavillon Charles X, a neo-classical building a few metres further along. It housed the steam-driven replacement machine in 1827 and is still being used as a water pumping station. There is a commemorative sign here with an evocative 18th-century painting showing the Machine and the aqueduct above it. To the right of the sign you can see an enormous series of pipes and one large one running straight up the hill you have just descended, following the path of the original Machine which was in use until 1817. It was replaced by steam-driven and then hydraulic versions. Since 1968 the water from the Seine has been pumped uphill by electric power and now supplies 22 *communes*, including Versailles.

The **259 bus** to Nanterre Préfecture from the stop 'La Machine' is a little further along on the left, just before a restaurant and a pedestrian crossing. However, the most interesting painter's **view** of the Machine de Marly is opposite the Pavillon Charles X, in the form of two reproductions of Sisley's paintings, one beside the riverside path and the other set back from the road, overlooking the water. It is worth crossing the busy road at this point, if you can, to see the one by the water's edge, *Barrage de la Machine dite de Marly*, 1876. The view of the river from here has changed only a little and the fascination of the spot for painters is instantly comprehensible. The low red-brick building in the middle of the water is a vestige of the 19th century hydraulic machine.

At this point you could return to Paris from the 259 bus stop 'La Machine' to your right on the other side of the road or continue along the river in the opposite direction to the next bridge, the Pont de Bougival. It is worth the walk if you are an Impressionist fan, interested in the history of Bougival or just want to continue walking, with a further walking option when you reach the bridge (see below). But be warned that the busy road beside the peaceful river is a constant reminder of how times have changed and if you are there on a Sunday you are most unlikely to find a café open.

Optional 1 km continuation of the walk to the Pont de Bougival

Bougival reached the height of its popularity as a riverside place for eating, drinking, boating and dancing and as an inspiration for artists during the 1880s, its atmosphere captured by perhaps the best-known Impressionist painting of them all, Renoir's *La Danse à Bougival*, 1883. The English artist Turner, often considered a forerunner of the Impressionists, first painted the Seine at Bougival in 1831 and was followed by Corot, Renoir, Monet, Pissarro, Sisley, Berthe Morisot and Vlaminck. Other famous Bougival residents included Mistinguett, the music hall star, Georges Bizet, the composer of *Carmen*, Ivan Turgenev and Alexandre Dumas *fils*.

There are five more reproductions of paintings along the river path to Bougival, by Sisley, Vlaminck, Pissarro and Turner, although they are fairly easy to miss as their backs are towards you. Continue along the river and cross the road at the bridge, where there is a well-established Moroccan restaurant, 'Le

'La Danse à Bougival', Pierre-Auguste Renoir, 1883

Maroc en Yvelines'. There is a *café-tabac* a little further along, behind the 'Pont de Bougival' **259 bus stop** for Nanterre.

If you want to continue walking there is an interesting **1 km detour** uphill via the first road to the right of the restaurant, the rue du Général Leclerc. It will take you to the heart of the old village of Bougival, which contains several cafés and is crowned by an impressive 13th century church, usually open.

Return to the river for the **259 bus to Nanterre Préfecture station**, or continue along the road past the café, crossing it at the Holiday Inn to follow the 3 km towpath walk along the Seine to Rueil-Malmaison station, described on p. 151.

Distance from Paris: 18 km (11 miles)
Depart: Gare St Lazare
Arrive: Marly-le-Roi
Journey time: 33 minutes
Length of visit: Half or full day
Return from: Bougival by 259 bus to RER Nanterre Préfecture
Alternative return from: Louveciennes or RER Rueil-Malmaison
Navigo Zone: 3
Single ticket: 4.95€
Distance from Marly-le-Roi station to Louveciennes church: 2.4 km (1½ miles)
Distance from Marly-le-Roi station to Louveciennes station: 3.4 km (2 miles)
Distance from Louveciennes church to Machine de Marly: 2 km (1 mile)
Distance from Machine de Marly to Pont de Bougival: 1 km (½ mile)
Distance from Maroc en Yvelines to Bougival church and back: 1.2 km (¾ mile)
Population: Marly-le-Roi, 16,485; Louveciennes, 7,059

Getting there

SNCF trains to Saint-Nom la Bret-èche Forêt de Marly, stopping at Marly-le-Roi, leave Gare St Lazare (*Île de France*) every half hour.

If you return from Louveciennes on the same line, trains run every half hour up to midnight, taking 30 minutes to St Lazare. If you return from Nanterre Préfecture, RER A trains run every 15 minutes up to midnight, taking 20 minutes or less to Châtelet-Les Halles.

The **259 bus** from Bougival runs daily at 10-20 minute intervals up to midnight, taking about 27 minutes to Nanterre Préfecture RER station. You can use a Paris métro ticket on this bus or buy a slightly more expensive ticket from the driver.

Car: A13, exit no. 6 towards Saint-Germain-en-Laye, RN 186 towards Marly-le-Roi.

RATP map *plan de secteur, no. 5* is useful for the Bougival part of this trip. See p. 179.

When to go

Mild sunny weather is preferable for this outdoor trip.

Useful information

Office de tourisme Marly-le-Roi, 2 avenue des Combattants, 78160 Marly-le-Roi, tel 01 30 61 61 35, www.saintgermainenlaye-tourisme.fr, info@seine-saintger main.fr. Open 2–6 pm on Wednesday, Thursday, Friday and public holidays, 10.30 am–12.30 pm and 2–6 pm at weekends in summer; in winter on Wednesdays 2–5pm and at weekends 11 am–1.30 pm and 2–5 pm. Closed on public holidays in winter.

Office de tourisme Bougival, 1 rue du Général Leclerc, 78380 Bougival, tel 01 39 69 21 23, www.tourisme-bougival.com. Open 10 am–12.30 pm on Tuesday, Wednesday and Saturday and 2.30–5.30 pm on weekdays.

Cafés

Le Narval *café-tabac*/brasserie 36 Grande Rue, Marly-le-Roi, tel 09 51 28 17 93. Open to 8.30 pm every day except Wednesday. Vietnamese specialities.

Café de la Mairie, 37 rue du Général Leclerc, 78430 Louve-ciennes, tel 01 30 82 24 42. Open to 3 pm or later Monday-Saturday, closed on Sunday.

Le Clemenceau *café-tabac/ brasserie*, 4 quai Georges Clemenceau, 78380 Bougival, tel 09 61 33 78 69. A little further along to the right of 'Maroc en Yvelines', behind the 259 bus stop. Open to 6.30 pm Monday–Saturday, closed on Sunday.

Restaurants

There are several restaurants in the Grande Rue at Marly-le-Roi although I have only tried one, usually preferring to picnic en route.

Le Village Grec, 1 bis, rue Guillaume Coustou, 78160 Marly-le-Roi, tel 01 39 69 04 32, https://le-village-grec.business.site. Open daily except Monday and on Sunday evening. This is the only Greek restaurant I have found which sells retsina by the glass. The food is nothing special but the atmosphere is convivial and the Greek coffee is good.

Getting around the Île de France

Getting into the local rhythm

Exploring the Île de France is an excellent education in itself about what makes France tick – literally. The timing of your trip should be in tune with the rhythm of French provincial life, particularly at lunchtimes, weekends and during holiday periods.

Opening hours: Local tourist offices and the smaller châteaux and museums tend to have extremely complicated schedules, varying according to the day of the week and the season, and are often closed for lunch. **The golden rule is *always* to phone before leaving** to check that the place you want to visit will be open. Phone, rather than check online, as websites and Google listings are not always up to date. If there is no answer from a château or museum try ringing the local *Mairie*—outside lunchtime, of course.

Restaurant opening hours outside Paris may be charmingly unpredictable, depending on the number of customers and the mood of the *patron*, as they are often family-run. They may be closed during school holidays, have changed owners and opening hours, or have closed down, so if you are planning to visit a particular restaurant, **always phone first** to check that it will be open.

Generally, restaurants are open at lunchtime from around 11.30 am to 3 pm, but it is risky to place your order after 1.30 pm. The best dishes, or worse still, the chef may have gone by then. Things are more relaxed on Sundays, when you might get away with turning up at 2 pm or even later. Evening opening times are from around 7.30 to 9.30 pm. Traditional French restaurants tend to be closed after about 3 pm on Sunday and at least one other day in the week, usually Monday.

You can generally get an omelette or a sandwich in a café at any time of the day during the week. On Sundays they tend to be foodless and may close distressingly early, at around 2 pm. In such cases, is quite acceptable to buy a sandwich at the local *boulangerie* and take it with you to eat in the café, ordering a drink to go with it. However, it is polite to ask if the café is selling sandwiches before heading to the baker, usually not far away.

Vegetarians are catered for better than they used to be, but if the menu contains nothing of interest to a vegetarian, ask if they can give you *une assiette de légumes*. It is usually good value.

Restaurant terms: *Menu* means a fixed price menu, usually three courses. Wine and coffee are rarely included. A *formule* is a two-course fixed price menu, usually a choice of a first and a main course (*entrée et plat*) or a main course and dessert (*plat et dessert*), sometimes including a glass of wine, beer or mineral water. The *plat du jour* is the dish of the day, usually part of the menu, and often a bargain in terms of quality and price. A *pichet* of wine is the house wine, served in 25cl or 50cl jugs (ask for *un quart* or *un demi*), varying greatly in quality depending on the restaurant. A *pichet* of a well-chosen *vin de pays* (local wine from a particular region) may be better value than an expensive but mediocre bottle. The French tend to go for Côtes du Rhône as a safe bet. A restaurant is legally obliged to serve you a jug of tap water free, if you ask for *une carafe d'eau, s'il vous plaît*. If you say *De l'eau, s'il vous plaît*, you are likely to get a bottle of expensive mineral water.

Weekends: Small towns in the Île de France tend to be very lively on Sunday mornings, when everyone is shopping for Sunday lunch until about 1 pm. In some villages this may also be the only time in the week when the church is open. Saturdays are also busy, but after about 3 pm on Sunday many of these places can seem deserted and you will probably be glad you are staying in Paris.

The pleasures of provincial life

Once you have adjusted to the local rhythm, you will start to appreciate the ways in which life is different, not only from other countries but from Paris as well.

People: People are generally much friendlier than in Paris and it is usual to greet the strangers you pass on a country walk, as well as the people you have commercial transactions with. The formula is 'Bonjour, m'sieur/madame', rather than just 'Bonjour', which is too abrupt. Occasionally, you may come across someone who treats you with provincial suspicion. Don't take it personally. Remember that you are not just a stranger (bad) but a foreigner (worse), and that even if you were French, it wouldn't make much difference. On the whole, people are extra helpful when they realise you are a foreigner because *any* visitor in some of these places is unusual and a foreign visitor is positively exotic.

Prices: Another pleasant difference is that café and restaurant prices tend to be as low as if you were in a province 300 km rather than just 30 km away from Paris. I always look for the cost of an ordinary cup of black coffee (*café express*) taken at the table (*salle*) as a fairly reliable indicator of the local prices. The Paris average is 2.50€ or more, so anything less than this is an encouraging sign.

Food: Not only are restaurant prices generally lower, the quality and quantity of the food are usually superior to Paris fare. A *kir* (apéritif) will be made with a decent wine rather than the cheapest plonk and the ingredients of the dishes are likely to be fresh and properly cooked, rather than frozen and microwaved. This is what French cooking is all about and you should take advantage of the generally non-commercial approach to order traditional dishes you don't often see on Paris menus.

The love of numbers

It may surprise you to know that the royal road to a successful career as a senior civil servant in France is an aptitude for mathematics, and state planning reflects this bias.

Administrative divisions: The entire country is divided into 22 *régions*, subdivided into 100 administrative *départements* which are known by numbers as well as by names. For example, the Île de France *région* consists of eight *départements*: Paris (75), Seine-et-Marne (77), Yvelines (78), Essonne (91), Hauts-de-Seine (92), Seine-St-Denis (93), Val-de-Marne (94) and Val-d'Oise (95). Every French schoolchild knows the *département* numbers, which always feature as the postcode in the address. For example, 75004 PARIS means the fourth *arrondissement* of the *département* of Paris. These divisions are deep in the national mindset. If you need to phone directory enquiries or ask about train timetables, the first question is likely to be 'In

what department?' and it helps if you can rattle off the number, or at least the name.

It is also helpful to keep administrative divisions in mind when reading tourist office maps and literature, which usually organise information on this principle. Likewise, stations outside the Île de France region are not shown on the Île de France railway map, so it is a good idea to take a Michelin or IGN map with you. The names of the stations, by the way, may consist of two place names, as in 'Moret – Veneux-Les-Sablons'. This means that they serve two *communes* (districts) and will usually be located in the middle, about two kilometres away from each of them.

The French attitude to information

French education, with its emphasis on the formal and abstract, has bred a horror of appearing to patronise people by over-simplifying or stating the obvious. This means that information is often not concrete or detailed enough to satisfy Anglophone tastes. Knowledge is also power, more than in most other countries, so it is rare to find an under-paid bureaucrat pressing more information on you than you have asked for.

As local tourist offices are often staffed by volunteers or employees of the *Mairie*, you should bear in mind that tourism is, understandably, usually fairly low on the local council's list of priorities and proceed accordingly. The secret is to know which questions to ask. If you can establish a rapport with the person you are dealing with, so much the better. Beginning with 'Bonjour, Madame/M'sieur' rather than 'Je veux savoir...' is a good start.

PRACTICAL DETAILS

Public transport in the Île de France

Paris is the hub of the Île de France train network, with suburban lines radiating in every direction for up to 80 kilometres. The region is divided into five concentric zones, with Paris itself in Zones One and Two, a radius of about 8 km from Notre Dame.

The RATP (*Régie autonome des transports parisiens*) is responsible for the métro, buses and trams within and often beyond this central zone and for the most heavily used suburban express trains, RER (*Réseau express régional*) lines A1, A2, A4 and B2 and B4, which cross central Paris, terminating up to 21 km away. The state-owned railway company, the SNCF (*Société nationale des chemins de fer français*) is responsible for the rest of the RER network and for all the suburban trains.

SNCF trains run on the left, as trains were first developed in Britain, and so do RER trains, as they have inherited the SNCF suburban network, whereas métro trains run on the right. Métro lines are usually referred to by numbers, such as 'Métro Line Seven', although people might also refer to them by destination, e.g. 'Villejuif' or 'Mairie d'Ivry', to indicate which branch they are referring to. But the RER is always referred to as RER A, RER B or even RER B4. These letters reflect the order in which each line was constructed, so RER E is the latest one.

The best large map of the system is the RATP *Plan de réseau Île de France (no. 1)*, available free from métro stations. Or download it from www.ratp.fr/plan-transilien.

Types of ticket

The streamlining of public transport in the Île de France under the umbrella of Île de France Mobilités means that you can buy a weekly or monthly *Navigo Découverte* pass at any métro or RER station, covering all forms of public transport in all five zones. Paris métro tickets are also valid on trams, RER trains within Paris (Zones 1–2) and all RATP buses, both within and outside Paris. You can buy a ticket to most SNCF or RER stations in the Île de France (Zones 3–5) from métro stations in central Paris and use it to cover the whole of your journey, including the métro.

In March 2022 the price of a single journey in the Île de France, excluding airport journeys, was capped at 5€, 4€ if you buy a *carnet* of 10 tickets for 40€. You will pay less than this for journeys in the zones closer to Paris, but never more. This generous change has effectively halved the cost of day-trips to Zone Five.

If you are staying **mainly in Paris** and will make only one or two journeys to the outer zones it is probably cheaper to buy single Métro tickets for 2.10€ or to buy a contact-less *Navigo Easy* pass and load it with ten métro tickets for 16.90€ and then buy separate tickets for travel beyond Zone Two, as and when you need them, from a métro station. That way, your métro journey is included in the price of the ticket.

Similar to the Oyster pass used in London, a plastic Navigo pass is validated simply by touching it against the electronic readers at the entrance to the train or métro station or the bus or tram. Navigo Easy has replaced the *carnet* of ten cardboard tickets and I have been reliably informed that it really is easy. It costs 2€ to buy the plastic pass online or at métro stations and *tabacs* or you can use the Bonjour RATP app to download it to your mobile phone for free. You then load it with the appropriate tickets. Visit www.ratp.fr/en/titres-et-tarifs/t-ticket-navigo-easy-pass-and-telephone for full details.

If you arrive at the beginning of the week and want to make **at least two return journeys beyond Paris**, especially if they are in Zone Five, a weekly *Navigo Découverte* could offer real savings. This pass, available for a week or a month, gives you unlimited travel by métro, train, bus and tram in all five zones, including airports, with the exception of Orlyval. Visit www.iledefrance-mobilites.fr/en/tickets-fares/detail/navigo-weekly-ticket for full details. It costs 5€ as it is designed to last for about ten years and you will need a passport-size photo. You then load it with the *Forfait Navigo Semaine, toutes zones*, which runs from Monday morning to Sunday evening and can be bought from Friday for the following week. It currently costs 30€.

It is probably a better deal than the one-, two-, three- and five-day visitor's pass, *Paris Visite*, which offers unlimited travel in Zones 1-3 or 1-5 and some rather limited reductions on entry to a few tourist attractions within and outside Paris. It currently costs 30.10€ for a three-day pass in Zones 1–3, 60.70€ for Zones 1–5. Visit www.iledefrance-mobilites.fr/en/tickets-fares/detail/paris-visite-ticket for details.

Another option is to buy the *Forfait Navigo Jour* which you can load onto your Navigo Easy account, a one-day pass allowing unlimited travel on all forms of public transport, except Orlyval. The price varies according to the number of zones, from 8.45€ for Zones 1–2 to 20.10€ for Zones 1-5. See www.ratp.fr/en/titres-et-tarifs/one-day-navigo-travel-pass for details.

Trains

Paris is not only the hub of the Île de France train network, it is also the hub of the national train network and a major international destination. Main line stations such as the Gare du Nord are intersections for the métro, the RER and for SNCF local, national and international trains. The following signs help you to navigate main line stations:

RER (pronounced 'air-er-air'): Suburban express trains. The five RER lines, A, B, C, D and E, cross Paris, converging at or near Châtelet-Les Halles and intersect with métro and SNCF stations. They are the most heavily-used commuter lines, especially line A. Underground in most of Paris, overground outside.

SNCF Transilien ('across the Île de France') or **Île de France**: Suburban trains, overground.

SNCF TER (*Transport express régional*): Regional trains.

SNCF Grandes Lignes: Main line trains to major cities in France and abroad.

TGV (*Trains à grande vitesse*): High speed trains to major cities in France and abroad.

The **frequency** of suburban trains depends on proximity to Paris. The RER and SNCF trains serving the inner suburbs generally run every 15 minutes, more often during the rush hour. Stations further away from Paris may only be served by trains every half hour or every hour. Sometimes the gaps between trains may be longer than this, although the frequency

of suburban trains has improved enormously in the last few years. Most trains run up to about midnight, but check return times for remoter destinations.

SNCF platforms: The main suburban departures board (*Départs transilien/Île de France*) shows the departure time of the train, its ultimate destination (*direction*) and the platform number (*voie*). So if you were going to La Ferté-sous-Jouarre, you would look for 'Château-Thierry' on the departure board. If you arrive with less than 15 minutes to spare, your train may no longer be shown. Don't panic – scan the platform departure boards for a train leaving at the right time and run your eye down the list of stations at which the train stops until you find the right one.

RER platforms: The platform display board shows the train's code name (e.g. NORA, ROMI) which refers to its destination and which stations it stops at. All the stations on the line are listed underneath but not all of them will be lit up or indicated by a white square next to the name, meaning that this train doesn't stop there. Wait until your station is indicated before getting on the train. On the way to remoter destinations on the RER C line the train may divide at certain stations and this will be indicated in sneaky smaller letters underneath the station name. If you are in any doubt, ask fellow-passengers if you are in the right carriage for your destination ('Ce train va-t-il à...?').

Information on train times and ticket prices

Websites

The RATP www.ratp.fr and the SNCF Île de France www.trans ilien.com websites both contain detailed information on train and bus times and prices in Paris and the Île de France, downloadable maps of the system, useful local maps and much else besides, in English as well as French. But I have found that the easiest and clearest website containing all this information is www.iledefrance-mobilites.fr/en.

Telephone

If you speak French (and even if you don't – some of the staff may speak English), you can ring the following numbers:

RATP, tel 34 24 (local call rate). Automated information on Paris and Île de France trains and buses, available Monday-Friday 7am-9pm, weekends 9am-5pm. Press 9 for English.

SNCF Transilien, tel 36 58 (local call rate). 24 hours a day, seven days a week, in French. Automated information on time-tables and ticket prices for the Île de France. If you want to speak to an adviser (*conseiller*), wait to the end of the recording.

SNCF tel 36 35 (local call rate). Daily 8 am-8 pm. Information and reservations for all SNCF trains including the Île de France. Press the hash key, followed by 85 to switch to this service in English.

You could even just turn up at the station without bothering to check the times beforehand. This is not as risky as it sounds, as there will usually be a train within 30 minutes if you arrive at about 10 am, even on a Sunday.

Train timetables

Ideally, you want a *fiche horaire*, a free pocket timetable to take with you, so that you can change your mind if necessary about which train to take back. You can get these from the relevant SNCF ticket office, either in Paris or at your destination and you may have to ask, as local timetables are rarely on display. SNCF train times change slightly every sum-mer and winter, so it is always worth having the latest one. You can also download timetables from www.transilien.com.

Buying a ticket from a machine

The simplest way to avoid queues at the ticket office or machines at busy main line stations is to buy your ticket from a **métro station machine**. This also saves you a métro ticket, as the métro journey is always included in the price of tickets for the Île de France. You have to use the machine, because métro stations no longer sell tick-ets. The staff in the ticket offices are there to supply information. The more central métro station ma-chines can issue tickets for most, although not all, destinations in the Île de France. They take credit cards or cash, some giving change.

The **RATP ticket machines** in métro stations are labelled *Tickets/ Navigo, RER, Métro, Tramways, Bus*. Most are touchscreens but some use a roller system for you to make your choice. You turn the roller to select English, validate by pressing the green button and then select 'Tickets for Paris region' (*Billets Île de France*). Validate and then turn the roller again to select the station you want in the Île de France, listed alphabetically.

For destinations in the Île de France which are not listed by the métro machines, use the touch-screen **SNCF Paris Île de France ticket machines** at main line stations, labelled *Tickets/Navigo, Train, RER, Bus, Tramway, Métro*. Touch the flag for English and select the option 'Tickets for Paris region'.

For destinations beyond the Île de France use the touchscreen **SNCF ticket machines** at main line stations labelled *Billets Grandes Lignes, Achat, retrait, échange* and choose English. You can of course also buy tickets from the ticket office, or online at www.sncf-connect. com/app/en-en/home/search.

On the way back you will probably have to buy your ticket from a machine, as many of the smaller stations in the Île de France are not staffed at weekends. These machines are usually located on the platform. Don't forget to validate your ticket by inserting it in the yellow *composteur* if the machine has not already date-stamped it for you.

NB: If the machine doesn't recognise your credit card do not try more than twice, as on the third failed try the machine will swallow it. I speak from experience.

It is no cheaper to buy a return ticket than a single, although it will save you from fiddling with the ticket machine on the way back. On the other hand, there may be a more interesting way back, via a different station, by bus or even by boat, so you might want to leave your options open. Be warned that if you do return from another station, even one in the same zone, a return ticket will not go through the machine, and it is not refundable.

Regulations and fines

There can be a certain arbitrariness in the way regulations are enforced in France, the good side of this being that your innocence or charm can sometimes melt an official. On the other hand, it is assumed that everyone knows the regulations, so they are rarely spelt out. I was told by my SNCF informant that if you plead ignorance it will be assumed that you are lying, as 'a French person who said they didn't know would probably be lying – and they can lie in the most convincing and charming way imaginable'. So for the benefit of innocent foreigners, here are the regulations:

Île de France train tickets are valid indefinitely, so it is up to you to demonstrate that you have no intention of using them more than once. You do this by inserting your ticket into one of the orange or yellow machines (*composteurs*) near the platform to be validated i.e. date-stamped before you get on the train. You validate a Navigo pass by touching it against the Navigo reader.

If you have not had time to validate your ticket, be warned that this can mean an on-the-spot fine of 50€. You can be fined 5€ if you have not validated your Navigo pass. Travelling without a ticket, for whatever reason, carries an on-the-spot fine of 50€. Putting your feet on the seats is fined at 50€ and smoking or vaping in a non-smoking area could set you back 68€. These lapses fall into the category of *infractions de comportement* (behavioural misdemeanours) which are viewed as seriously as travelling ticketless, although you will see people cheerfully infringing these 'rules' all the time.

If you have not had time to buy or to validate your ticket, it is in your interest to show your *bonne foi* (good faith) by approaching the inspector or guard (*le contrôleur, le chef de bord*) as soon as possible after getting on the train. You are then unlikely to be fined, merely charged the cost of the ticket if you haven't got one.

Buses

In general, trains are the main form of public transport outside Paris, buses being regarded as plugs to fill the gaps in the train service.

RATP buses linking the inner suburbs to Paris may offer a more adventurous, although slower, alternative to the train. See the maps section on pp. 178-179 for details of how to get hold of local bus maps, *plans de secteurs, nos. 4-14*. You can also consult **bus timetables and maps** on the RATP and SNCF websites and on www.iledefrance-mobilites.fr/en. You can use your Navigo or a Paris métro ticket on all RATP buses.

Local bus services linking rural *communes* are geared to local needs, so they do not usually operate at weekends or during school holidays. Even if they do, the gaps in the service are so long that you would probably be better off walking or taking a taxi. You can check the current dates for school holidays in the Paris region (zone C) on www.education.gouv.fr/pid250 58/le-calendrier-scolaire.html.

Taxis

Uber may be the quickest way to find an available taxi. Otherwise, it is a good idea to Google taxis in the area beforehand (it will help if you know the local postcode, shown in the first address given at the end of each chapter in this book) and book one online, or ring the local tourist office and ask them to book one for you. You can of course ring for a taxi yourself when you need one but be warned that it may take some time to find one which is available. Prices tend to be higher than in Paris, as you are also paying for the driver to come and pick you up.

Boats

There are some interesting local boat trips on the 724 km of canals and rivers in the Île de France, such as the one along the Canal de l'Ourcq described in the visit to La Ferté Milon in *An Hour From Paris*. Visit www.paris.fr/pages/tmp-canaux-7834 and scroll down to *Le tourisme fluvial* to see a selection. It is always worth asking the local tourist office about boat trips in the area, as new ones may have started up. Apart from a few well-established names like Canauxrama, companies tend to be very small and local and publicity is not their strong point. **Always phone to check** the times and dates in any leaflet you are given before setting out.

An excellent free **map** of the 130-kilometre long canal network, *Carte du réseau fluvial de la Ville de Paris*, can be sent to you by the Mairie de Paris, Services des Canaux, 62 Quai de la Marne, 75019 Paris, tel 01 44 89 14 14, or email canaux.usagers@paris.fr. You can download it from www.paris.fr/pages/tmp-canaux-7834.

Bicycles

Information on Vélib, the bicycle rental scheme in and around Paris, is available in French and English on the website www.velib-metropole.fr/en/map. More information on cycling in Paris is available in English on https://en.parisinfo.com/what-to-see-in-paris/info/guides/paris-cycling-exploring. You can view an interactive cycling map of the Île de France on https://velo.smartidf.services/ (in French) or buy the IGN map, *Île de France by bike*, on a scale of 1 cm to 1 km.

Walking

There are several walking guides to the Île de France for the serious rambler/hiker, available in French.

For the non-serious walker, at whom this guide is aimed, it is useful to know that the FFRP (*Féderation française de la randonnée pédestre*) www.ffrandonnee.fr/, the French version of the Ramblers' Association, has a system of letters and coloured markings (*le balisage*) which help you to find your way across country (see opposite). These waymarked footpaths are shown on the IGN (*Institut géographique national*) large-scale TOP 25 maps.

Footpaths are classified as follows:

GR (*Grande randonnée*): Major linear footpath crossing several regions. Red and white stripe at eye level along the route, red on IGN maps.

GRP (*Grande randonnée de pays*): Major footpath circling an entire region. Red and yellow stripe along the route, red on IGN maps.

PR (*Promenade et randonnée*): Shorter circular routes taking one to eight hours. Yellow stripe along the route, red on IGN maps.

One or two horizontal stripes mean you are on the right path, a horizontal stripe above a right or left angle means turn right or left at the next fork and a St Andrew's cross means you will stray off the path if you take this route. More unusually, two horizontal stripes with a vertical line through them indicate that the path is a way-marked deviation from the main one.

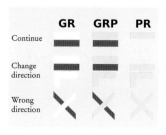

The red and white or yellow markings are deliberately rather discreet, usually painted at eye level on a tree or lamp-post. However, once you start looking for them you will notice them everywhere, including central Paris. It is generally a good idea to follow the FFRP paths, which avoid busy roads as far as possible, sometimes leading to an unsuspected underpass or taking you through a pretty wood.

Maps

Regional maps: The clearest overall map of the Paris region is the **Michelin no. 106,** *Environs de Paris* which covers 40–80 km around Paris, on a scale of 1 cm to 1 km. Railway lines are shown, but you need practice to identify the tiny white square which indicates a railway station, as their names are not given. The version covering the whole of the Île de France is no. 514 on a scale of 1 cm to 2 km.

By far the most useful map for public transport users is the **RATP** *Plan de réseau Île de France (no. 1)* which shows the entire SNCF/RER train network for Paris and the Île de France, a radius of up to 80 kilometres from Paris. A version of it is reproduced at the front of this book. You could pick up the *Plan de Paris avec rues (no. 2)* at the same time, much more comprehensive than the maps aimed at tourists, which shows bus, métro, tram and train routes against a background of main street names and green spaces. These maps are available free from most métro and main line stations and can be downloaded from www.ratp.fr/plans-secteur.

Local maps: The **IGN** *Cartes Topographiques 25* on a scale of 1 cm to 250 metres are the French equivalent of the Ordnance Survey maps. They cover an area of around 250 square kilometres and cost about 12.75€ but are worth investing in if you want to do a lot of country walking in that particular area as they show the GR and PR footpaths very clearly. I have made rewarding discoveries, such as the walk from Meaux along the Canal de Chalifert to Esbly, by carefully studying the IGN map. Station and street names are not shown, but the online versions at www.geoportail.fr will show this level of detail if you go to *Fonds de carte*, select *OpenStreetMap monde* and zoom. These maps are far more useful to walkers than Google maps and can be printed out or shared. The RATP and SNCF websites can also display local maps for your destination, as can www.ilede france-mobilites.fr.

The free **Géoportail app** is invaluable to have on your phone, even if you have the relevant paper map with you. Select *carte topographique IGN* as the *fonds de carte* to match the map in your hand and see exactly where you are, with the added advantage of being able to zoom, at which point the map switches to *OpenStreetMap monde* to display the street names. Of course, it takes some of the fun out of getting lost and a paper map is still useful for an overview of where you are going.

The excellent free **RATP** *plans de secteur (nos. 4–14)* of the inner suburbs are by far the most useful of the local maps for public transport users, on a scale of 1.5 cm to 250 metres. They cover 11 areas within a radius of about 20 kilometres of Paris and clearly show all bus, train and tram routes against the physical background, including main street names. For example, no. 12 covers the Val-de-Marne area. It is well worth asking for these at the local train station for the area which interests you. The full set is available at the *Services* desk inside Châtelet-Les Halles station. However, be prepared for blank looks at other Paris stations, as people rarely ask for them and not many *Franciliens* seem to be aware of their existence. You can download them from www.ratp.fr/plans-secteur. You can also now download *plans de secteur* for the whole of the Île de France, nos. 15-72, from https://data.iledefrance-mobilites.fr/explore/dataset/plans-de-secteur/table/?disjunctive.departement&sort=numero_secteur.

Local tourist office maps vary enormously in detail and usefulness – some leave out little details such as the railway station or the scale – but they show street names as well as local phone numbers and they do give you an immediate impression of the spirit of the place you are visiting and its priorities.

Other useful sources of information

The **Paris Office du Tourisme et des Congrès** is at the Mairie de Paris, Hotel de Ville, 29 rue de Rivoli, 75004 Paris, tel 01 42 76 43 43, métro Hotel de Ville. Open daily 10 am to 6 pm. You can pick up a free city guide and map of Paris and a few leaflets and buy museum and theatre tickets here, as well as the *Paris Visite* pass. They also have information desks at Gare du Nord and the Carrousel du Louvre. Their comprehensive website www.parisinfo.com contains practical information in French and English on all aspects of visiting Paris, with lists of addresses.

The Paris region tourist office has information desks at Orly and Charles de Gaulle airports, Galeries Lafayette Homme and Disneyland Paris but no longer produces paper brochures. Their website www.visitparisregion.com

includes downloadable information in French and English on current cultural events in Paris and the Île de France.

For excellent detailed specialist studies, maps and up to date statistical information on the Île de France, some of it in English, visit the little-known and helpful urban development agency, **L'Institut Paris Region** at https://en.institut parisregion.fr.

Enlarge Your Paris www.en largeyourparis.fr is a website devoted to cultural and leisure activities in the newly baptised region of 'Grand Paris' (Greater Paris). You can sign up for their weekly newsletter, in French. The cultural activities tend to be in the suburbs closest to Paris but there are suggestions for walks further afield accessible by public transport, in partnership with **Helloways**, https://www.hello ways.com/en/, a website in French and English with downloadable walks covering some French cities including Paris. Their walks are beautifully photographed but I have found them rather low on useful detail.

Explore Paris https://explore paris.com/en/ is a partnership of Paris and local tourist offices offering guided visits and walks in French, some free, in Paris and up to about 20 km around Paris. The free ones are worth a try and the ones involving boating or boat trips are usually good value.

Books

In English

Ardagh, John, *France in the New Century*, Penguin 2000. Comprehensive and lively overview of post-war France, economic, social, cultural and political. Especially good on the relationship between Paris and the *banlieue* and on France's treatment of ethnic minorities. Out of print but available on Amazon and still the best overview I have read.

Michelin Green Guide series, *Northern France and the Paris Region*, 2017. Concise, attractive descriptions of the main places of interest en route for car drivers heading to Paris from England. It covers the better-known places in the Île de France, very much from a driver's point of view.

Platt, Polly, *French or Foe?* Culture Crossings 1994, third edition (UK), 2003. Aimed at Anglophones working for multinational companies in France, a still accurate and highly readable guide to cultural differences. Out of print but available on Amazon and the book I wish had existed when I arrived in Paris in 1991. I would still recommend it to new residents.

In French

Michelin Guides Verts series, *Île de France, Escapade à Chartres*, 2021. Concise but comprehensive and covers far more of the Île de France than the English version, *Northern France and the Paris Region*. Includes brief details of access by public transport for most of the visits. Heavy to carry around but a good reference book.

Murat, Inès, *Colbert*, Fayard, 1980. A well-written, although probably biased biography of Louis XIV's great minister (the author is one of Colbert's descendants), very useful to an understanding of modern France.

Bookshops

Smith and Son, 248 rue de Rivoli, 75001 Paris, tel 01 53 45 84 40, www.smithandson.com. Métro Concorde. Monday-Saturday 9.30 am–7.30 pm, Sunday 12.30–7 pm. The biggest selection in Paris of maps, guides and books in English. Its famous tea-room, where apparently Anaïs Nin used to meet her lovers, re-opened in 2016 after an absence of 26 years.

Gibert Joseph, ground floor, 26 Boulevard St Michel, 75006 Paris, tel 01 44 41 88 88, www.gibert.com/stores/paris-vi-gibert-joseph-librairie. Métro St Michel. Monday-Saturday 10 am-7.30 pm. University bookshop selling a range of maps and guides, mostly in French. Some are recent second-hand copies, marked 'occasion'.

Au Vieux Campeur Cartothèque, 2 rue de Latran, 75005, tel 01 53 10 48 27, www.auvieuxcampeur.fr/librairie/cartes/france. Métro Maubert-Mutualité. Monday to Friday, 11 am–7.30 pm, closes 9 pm on Thursday, Saturday 10 am–7.30 pm. The best range of IGN maps and a selection of other maps and guides, mainly in French.

Best days to visit

	Markets	*Châteaux/museums*
MONDAY		Musée Bossuet, Meaux (summer) Musée de Sèvres, Parc Saint-Cloud Château de Vincennes Château de Malmaison
TUESDAY	Rueil (Malmaison)	Château de Vincennes Crypts, Jouarre (afternoon, summer)
WEDNESDAY	Lagny	Musée Bossuet, Meaux Crypts, Jouarre Château de Vincennes Château de Malmaison Musée de Sèvres, Parc Saint-Cloud Musée Historique, Parc Saint-Cloud (afternoon, summer)
THURSDAY		Musée Bossuet, Meaux Crypts, Jouarre Château de Vincennes Château de Malmaison Musée de Sèvres, Parc Saint-Cloud
FRIDAY	Lagny	Musée Bossuet, Meaux Crypts, Jouarre Château de Vincennes Château de Malmaison Musée de Sèvres, Parc Saint-Cloud

	*Market*s	*Châteaux/museums*

SATURDAY	Meaux
	Rueil
	  (Malmaison)
		Pavillon Maurouard, Parc de la Poudrerie
		Musée Bossuet, Meaux
		Crypts, Jouarre
		Maison Hugo, Igny (summer)
		Château de Vincennes
		Château de Malmaison
		Musée de Sèvres, Parc Saint-Cloud
		Musée Historique, Parc Saint-Cloud
		  (summer, phone to check)
		Maison Caillebotte, Brunoy (afternoon)

SUNDAY	Lagny
	La Ferté-
	  sous-Jouarre
		Musée des Poudres, Parc de la Poudrerie
		  (spring and autumn)
		Pavillon Maurouard, Parc de la Poudrerie
		Musée Bossuet, Meaux
		  (free on first Sunday of month)
		Crypts, Jouarre (morning, summer)
		Maison Hugo, Igny (summer)
		Château de Vincennes
		  (free on 1st Sunday of month in winter)
		Château de Malmaison
		  (free on 1st Sunday of month)
		Musée de Sèvres, Parc Saint-Cloud
		  (free on 1st Sunday of month)
		Musée Historique, Parc Saint-Cloud
		  (summer, phone to check)
		Maison Caillebotte, Brunoy
		(afternoon)

General glossary

abbaye abbey
aire de jeux playground
alimentation grocery store
auberge inn

bac ferry
baignade bathing place (river, lake)
bal-musette dance with accordion music
banlieue suburb
barrage weir/dam
bar-tabac café/tobacconist
bistro(t) modest restaurant
bois wood(s)
brasserie café/restaurant serving meals or snacks throughout the day
boulangerie baker's shop
boules bowls (game)
buvette drinks stall

café-tabac café licensed to sell stamps and tobacco
camping camp/caravan site
car (autocar) coach
carte map, menu (à la carte)
cascades waterfall
château castle, palace, stately home, mansion, manor
château d'eau water tower
château fort fortified castle
château de plaisance stately home
chaumière (thatched) cottage
chemin path, lane
chemin de halage towpath
cimetière cemetery
commune urban or rural district, the smallest administrative unit
Conseil Council
couvent convent, monastery
curé priest

département administrative area, usually smaller than an English county
donjon keep, donjon
douves moat

écluse lock (canal)
école school
église church
exposition exhibition

ferme farm
férié, jour férié public holiday
fête festival, celebration
forêt forest
formule (restaurant) starter and main course or main course and dessert
fosse (la) pit
fossé (le) ditch
France profonde deepest France
fromager cheesemonger

gendarmerie police station
goûter children's afternoon snack
guinguette open air restaurant with dance floor, usually by a river
grand(e) great, important, big, tall
grille gate

hôpital hospital
hôtel de ville town or city hall

île island
îlot islet

jardin public public garden, park
jardin à l'anglaise landscaped garden
jardin à la française formal garden

jardin potager vegetable garden

kir aperitif made with wine and
fruit liqueur

lac lake
lavoir former public washhouse
next to stream or river
lycée grammar/high school

mairie town or city hall
maison de retraite retirement
home
marché market
menu set menu, usually of three
courses
merguez North African spicy
mutton sausages, popular in
couscous and at barbecues
moules frites mussels and chips, a
popular Belgian dish
moulin mill
musée museum

navette shuttle bus

office de tourisme tourist office

palais palace
parc park
parking car-park
passage à niveau level-crossing
passerelle foot-bridge
patron(ne) proprietor, boss
pavillon detached house, lodge
pays country, region, district
(*spécialités de pays*—local
specialities)
pétanque petanque (bowls)
pichet jug (of house wine)
piéton pedestrian
piscine swimming pool
place square
plage beach

plan map, plan
plat du jour dish of the day
PMU Pari mutuel urbain, a *café*
or *tabac* where people can bet
on horse races ('*pari mutuel*',
equivalent to the Tote)
pont bridge
porte gate, door, porch
Poste Post Office
préfecture administrative headquarters of a *département*
prieuré priory

radeau raft
randonnée pedestre walk, hike
région administrative area, larger
than an English county, consisting of several *départements*
remparts ramparts
réseau network
résidence secondaire 'second
home', country house
ruelle alley, lane
ru brook

salon de thé tea-room
sanitaires wc
sente path, footpath
sentier path, footpath
siècle century
spectacle show, entertainment
stade stadium, sports ground
syndicat d'initiative small tourist
office

tabac tobacconist
table d'orientation viewing table
tarif réduit concessions
tennis tennis courts
terrain de sport sports ground
terrasse terrace (in a café, refers
to the tables outside)
toilettes (les) wc
tour tower

Train traveller's glossary

Buying your ticket

ticket *billet*
ticket-office *billetterie/vente de billets*
suburban ticket-office *billets banlieue/Transilien/Île de France*
ticket-office window *guichet*
single ticket *aller simple*
return ticket *aller retour*
suburban ticket *billet Île de France*
A single ticket to…
  Un aller simple pour…
I would like to go to…
  Je voudrais aller à…
timetable/schedule *horaire*
pocket timetable *fiche horaire*
Have you got a timetable for…?
  Avez-vous une fiche horaire pour…?
fare *tarif*
half-fare *demi-tarif*
travel pass (weekly, monthly)
  Un passe Navigo Découverte (semaine, mois)
A top-up for zones 1 and 2
  Un forfait Navigo pour Paris (zones une et deux)
What time does it leave/arrive?
  Il part/arrive à quelle heure?
Does this train go to…?
  *Ce train va-t-il à…?/
  Ce train dessert-il…?*
I want to get off at…
  Je veux descendre à…

In general

à l'approche (train) approaching
arrêt stop/halt (as opposed to a proper station)
arrivées arrivals
chef de train/bord guard
compostez votre billet validate your ticket
composteur ticket validating machine
contrôleur ticket inspector
correspondance/changement change trains/intersection/transfer
départs banlieue/Île de France/Transilien suburban departures
direction destination
gare railway station
gare routière bus/coach station
grève strike
mouvement social industrial action
omnibus stopping train
perturbé disrupted
repère platform marker
retardé delayed
quai platform
queue du train back of the train/last carriage
sortie exit
tête du train front of the train/first carriage
train court/long short/long train
Ce train dessert…
  This train stops at…
voie track/platform
voiture carriage/car
voyageur passenger
Que tous les voyageurs descendent du train All change

Chronology of French rulers

*Names in **bold** are mentioned in the text*

Merovingians	*(481-751)*	*Bourbons*	
Clovis	481-511	**Henri IV**	1589-1610
		Louis XIII	1610-1643
Carolingians	*(751-987)*	**Louis XIV**	1643-1715
Pépin le Bref	751-768	**Louis XV**	1715-1774
Charlemagne	768-814	Louis XVI	1774-1792
		Louis XVII	(never reigned)
Capetians			
Hugues Capet	987-996	*First Republic*	
Robert II (le Pieux)	996-1031	*National Convention*	1792-1795
Henri I	1031-1060	*Directory*	1795-1799
Philippe I	1060-1108	*Consulate*	1799-1804
Louis VI	1108-1137		
Louis VII	1137-1180	*First Empire*	
Philippe Auguste	1180-1223	**Napoléon I**	1804-1814
Louis VIII	1223-1226		
Louis IX (St Louis)	1226-1270	*Restoration*	
Philippe III	1270-1285	Louis XVIII	1814-1824
Philippe IV (le Bel)	1285-1314	**Charles X**	1824-1830
Louis X	1314-1316		
Philippe V	1316-1322	*Constitutional monarchy*	
Charles IV	1322-1328	Louis Philippe	1830-1848
Valois		*Second Republic*	1848-1852
Philippe VI	1328-1350		
Jean II (le Bon)	1350-1364	*Second Empire*	
Charles V (le Sage)	1364-1380	**Napoléon III**	1852-1870
Charles VI	1380-1422		
Charles VII	1422-1461	*Third Republic*	1870-1940
Louis XI	1461-1483		
Charles VIII	1483-1498	*Vichy government*	1940-1944
Louis XII	1498-1515		
François I	1515-1547	*Provisional government*	
Henri II	1547-1559		1944-1946
François II	1559-1560		
Charles IX	1560-1574	*Fourth Republic*	1946-1958
Henri III	1574-1589		
		Fifth Republic	1958 to present

Acknowledgements

Special thanks to Joan Fleming for her engaging company on many walks and her discovery of Brunoy, and to both her and my sister Kate Turner for their unfailingly constructive suggestions and support, to Amanda Metcalf-Menguelti, Patricia Plénier, Saara Marchadour, Lesann Caldwell and Denis Cohadon for their cheerful and helpful company while revising these walks, to François Portier for suggesting Louveciennes and to Dewi Jones for suggesting the Parc de la Poudrerie.

My grateful thanks, as ever, to Alexander Fyjis-Walker and Patrick Davies at Pallas Athene for their invaluable professional support.

Picture credits

Index

Agincourt, battle of 118
Auvers-sur-Oise 24
banlieue 29–31, 36, 40–44
Barbizon 29
Berlioz, Hector (1803–1869) 110
Bertin, Louis-François
    (1766–1841) 110
Bièvre, river 106–112
Bièvres 109
Bizet, Georges (1838–1875) 144,
    151–152, 164
Blum, Léon (1872–1950) 108
boats 176–177
    rowing boats for hire, Bois de
    Vincennes 124, Yerres 105
books 180–181
bookshops 181
Bossuet, Jacques (1627–1704)
    71-72, 73–74
Bougival 151–152, 164–167
Brie 32, 68, 71
    cheese 72
Brunoy 98–101
buses 176
Bussy-St-Georges 30, 32
Caesar, Julius 37
Caillebotte, Gustave (1848–1894)
    98, 104
canals
    map 177
    Canal de Chalifert 24, 37, 44,
    71, 76–79
    Canal de Chelles 38, 90, 94–95
    Canal de l'Ourcq 32, 36, 50,
    52, 56
Capet Hugues (r. 987–996) 38, 187
Carné, Marcel (1906–1996) 91
Cergy 30, 32
Champagne 59, 60, 71, 116
Champigny 91
Chantilly 31

Charles V (r. 1364–1380) 117–118,
    122, 187
Charles VII (r. 1422–1461) 62,
    187
Charles X (r. 1824–1830) 139, 187
Chateaubriand, François-René de
    (1768–1848) 110
châteaux in Île de France 34
    Bagatelle 137, 138, 141
    Bois-Préau 149
    Fontainebleau 29, 34
    Malmaison 144–149, 153–154
    Marly 31, 155–156
    Rambouillet 31, 147
    des Roches 106, 110, 115
    Saint-Cloud 130–131, 133
    Versailles 24, 31, 130, 155, 156,
    163
    Vincennes 24, 39, 116–127
Chénier, André (1762–1794) 157
Chevreuse 31
Chirac, Jacques (1932–2019) 40
churches of historic interest:
    Lagny-sur-Marne 59, 60, 62–64
    Meaux, cathedral 71, 73
    Mareuil-lès-Meaux 77
    Jouarre 81, 84–87, 88–89
    Brunoy 99
    Yerres 105
    Jouy-en-Josas 106, 113–114
    Château de Vincennes 118, 122
    Saint-Cloud 134
    Rueil 150
    Marly-le-Roi 157–159,
    Louveciennes 160
    Bougival 165
Clichy-sous-Bois 49
Clovis (r. 486–511) 38, 134, 187
Conflans-Sainte-Honorine 23
Colbert, Jean-Baptiste (1619–
    1683) 181

Corot, Camille (1796–1875) 110, 164

cycling 177

Dagobert I (r. 629–639) 81, 187

dancing 90–93

De Beauharnais, Hortense (1783–1837) 150

De Gaulle, Charles (1890–1970) 119

Diderot, Denis (1713–1784) 118

Disneyland (Paris) 32, 59, 67, 68

Du Barry, Madame (1743–1793) 157, 162

Dumas, Alexandre (*fils*) (1824–1895) 164

Esbly 71, 74, 76, 78

Evry 30, 31, 32

FFRP 34, 177–178

Fontaine, Pierre-François Léonard (1762–1853) 145

Fontainebleau, forest 34

Footpaths 177–178

Fouquet, Nicolas (1615–1680) 118

Gaul 38

Glossary general 184–185
    trains 186

Grand Morin, river 78

Grand Paris 41–44

guinguettes 33, 44, 90–94, 97

Gounod, Charles (1818–1893) 110, 134

Henri IV (r. 1589–1610) 118, 187

Henry V of England (r. 1413–1422) 118

Hertford, Richard, fourth Marquess of (1800–1870) 139

Houellebecq, Michel (b. 1956) 72

Hugo, Victor (1802–1885) 106, 108, 110

Hundred Years' War 117

Institut géographique national (IGN) 177, 181

Igny 24, 34, 36, 106–115

Île de France
    general 24, 29–31
    history and future 32–44
    practical information 168–181

Île du Martin-Pêcheur 91–92

Île Séguin 129

Impressionists 98, 104, 144, 155, 157, 164
    Neo-Impressionists at Lagny 59, 62, 64

Ingres, Jean-Auguste-Dominique (1780–1867) 110

Jacquerie, the 76, 117

Jean II (r. 1350–1364) 117, 187

Joan of Arc (1412–1431) 62, 63

Joinville 90, 91

Josephine, Empress (1763–1814) 144–151

Jouarre 81, 83–87

Jouy-en-Josas 34, 106, 107–108, 112–115
    toile de Jouy 107–108, 112

La Défense 30, 162

La Ferté-sous-Jouarre 24, 37, 39, 80–89

Lagny-sur-Marne 24, 27, 37, 39, 44, 59–70

lavoirs 64

Leconte de Lisle, Charles Marie René (1818–1894) 157

Le Nôtre, André (1613–1700) 74, 118, 130

Le Vau, Louis (1612–1670) 118

Liszt, Franz (1811–1886) 110

Louis IX (r. 1226–1270) 122, 187

Louis XIV (r. 1643–1715) 118, 130, 155–156, 157, 159, 181, 187

Louis XV (r. 1715–1774) 157, 159, 187

Louveciennes 34, 155, 156, 157, 160–162

Lutetia 106

Maillol, Aristide (1861–1944) 157

Malmaison 24, 36, 144–154

Mansart, Jules Hardouin (1646–1708) 130, 155, 156, 157

maps 45, 170, 171, 177, 178–179, 181

Marcel, Etienne (c. 1305–1358) 117

Mareuil-lès-Meaux 77

Marie-Antoinette (1755–1793) 113, 131, 139

Mariette, Auguste (1821–1881) 159
Markets, best days to visit 182–183
  Lagny-sur-Marne 60, 69
  La Ferté-sous-Jouarre 83
  Meaux 76
  Rueil 151
Marly-le-Roi 24, 31, 34, 36,
  155–167
Machine de Marly 155, 156,
  162–164
Marne-la-Vallée 32, 59, 68
Marne, river 32, 33, 37, 59, 65–67,
  68, 71, 76, 77–78, 80, 83, 84,
  87, 88, 90, 93, 94
  battles of the 83, 84
Meaux 24, 37, 39, 44, 71–79
Merovingians, the 81, 85, 187
Melun-Sénart 32, forest 98
Mirabeau, Comte de (1749–1791)
  118
Mistinguett (1875–1956) 164
Monet, Claude (1840–1926) 151,
  164
Mont-Valérien fort 131
Morisot, Berthe (1841–1895) 164
museums, best days to visit
  182–183
  Château de Malmaison 145–147
  Château de Vincennes 121–122
  Maison Caillebotte 103–104, 105
  Maison littéraire de Victor
    Hugo 110
  Merovingian crypts 85–87
  Musée Bossuet 73
  Musée Historique 133, 136
  Musée des Poudres 54
  Musée de Sèvres 128, 129, 136
  Pavillon Maurouard 53
Nanterre Préfecture 149, 153, 163,
  166
Napoleon I (r. 1804–1814) 84, 113,
  118, 131, 144–147, 150, 187
Napoleon III (r. 1852–1870) 131,
  150
Navigo 29
  practical information 45, 47,
    171–172

Neo-Impressionists
  See Impressionists
Neolithic, menhir 100–101
Neuilly-sur-Marne 24, 33, 36, 44,
  90–97
Nogent-sur-Marne 116, 126
Nin, Anaïs (1903–1977) 157, 161,
  181
Noisy-le-Grand 30, 31
Oberkampf, Christophe-Philippe
  (1738–1815) 106, 107–108,
  112–113
Oise, river 37
Orléans, Philippe d' (1640–1701)
  130
parks and gardens
  Bois de Boulogne 36, 137, 139
  Bois de Vincennes 36, 116
  Château de Malmaison 147–
    149
  Château des Roches 110
  Jardin de Bossuet 73–74
  Jardin de Trocadéro 128, 133,
    134
  Jardin Tropical, Bois de
    Vincennes 119–120, 124
  Maison Caillebotte 103–104,
    105
  Parc de Bagatelle, Bois de
    Boulogne 24, 137–143
  Parc de Bois-Préau 149
  Parc de Marly 31, 155–156,
    159–160
  Parc de la Poudrerie 24, 35, 36,
    44, 49–57
  Parc de Sceaux 31
  Parc Saint-Cloud 31, 128, 129,
    130, 131–134, 136
Pays de France 37
Percier, Charles (1764–1838) 145
Petit Morin, river 80, 83, 84, 87
Petitot, Emile (1838–1916) 77
Piaf, Edith (1915–1963) 91
Pissarro, Camille (1830–1903) 157,
  161, 164
Rabelais, François (1494–1553)
  110

Rambouillet 31, 145, 147
RATP 67
  practical information 45, 47,
  171–176
Redouté, Pierre Joseph (1759–
  1840) 147
Renoir, Pierre-Auguste (1841–
  1919) 157, 161, 164
RER 32, 40, 42, 43, 59, practical
  information 171–176
restaurants, general 168–170
  recommended :
  Le Saint Furcy, Lagny-sur-
    Marne 69
  L'Île des Cygnes, Condé Ste
    Libiaire 77–78, 79
  Chez Fifi, Neuilly-sur-Marne
    93–94, 97
  Le Pavillon de l'Île, Brunoy
    99–100, 105
  Château des Roches *salon de
    thé*, Bièvres 110, 115
  Robin des Bois, Jouy-en-Josas
    114, 115
  Le Terminus Château,
    Vincennes 116, 123, 127
  Le Village Grec, Marly-le-Roi
    159, 167
  Le Beauharnais, Rueil 151, 154
Retz, Cardinal de (1613–1679) 118
Ronsard, Pierre (1524–1585) 77
Rousseau, Jean-Jacques (1712–
  1778) 110
Rueil 144, 149–151
Rueil-Malmaison 152, 166
Sade, Marquis de (1740–1814)
  118, 122
St Adon 81, 85
St Agilbert 85
St Clodoald 134
Saint-Cloud 128, 134
Saint-Denis 32, 37, basilica 85
St Furcy 60, 63
Saint-Germain-en-Laye 31, 151
Saint-Quentin-en-Yvelines 32
St Ozanne 85
St Telchide 85

Sarcelles 32
Sardou, Victorien (1831–1908) 159
Satie, Erik (1866–1925) 110
Seine, river 37, 90, 106, 107, 116,
  128, 151, 156, 161, 162–166
Senlis 31, 38
Simenon, Georges (1903–1989) 91
Sisley, Alfred (1839–1899) 157,
  159, 160, 162, 163, 164
SNCF 32, 112
  practical information 45–47,
  171–176
taxis 176
trains 31, 43
  practical information 45–47,
  171–176, glossary 186
Turgenev, Ivan (1818–1883) 164
Turner, J. M. W. (1775–1851) 164
Vauboyen 106, 110
Versailles, Château de – see
  châteaux in Île de France
  town 24, 29, 31, 107, 118, 130,
  155, 156, 163
Vigée-Lebrun, Elisabeth (1755–
  1842) 157, 161
Vikings, the 38, 60
Villeparisis 44, 56
Viollet-le-Duc, Eugène (1814–
  1879) 118
Vlaminck, Maurice de (1876–1958)
  164
Voltaire (1694–1778) 118
walking 177–178
  maps 178–179
walks, optional additions to visits :
  Parc de la Poudrerie 56
  Lagny-sur-Marne 65
  Meaux 76
  Neuilly-sur-Marne 96
  Igny 108, 112
  Vincennes 124
  Malmaison 149, 151
  Marly-le-Roi 161, 164, 165, 166
Wallace, Sir Richard (1818–1890)
  139
Weill, Kurt (1900–1950) 157
Yerres 105, river 98, 99, 100–103